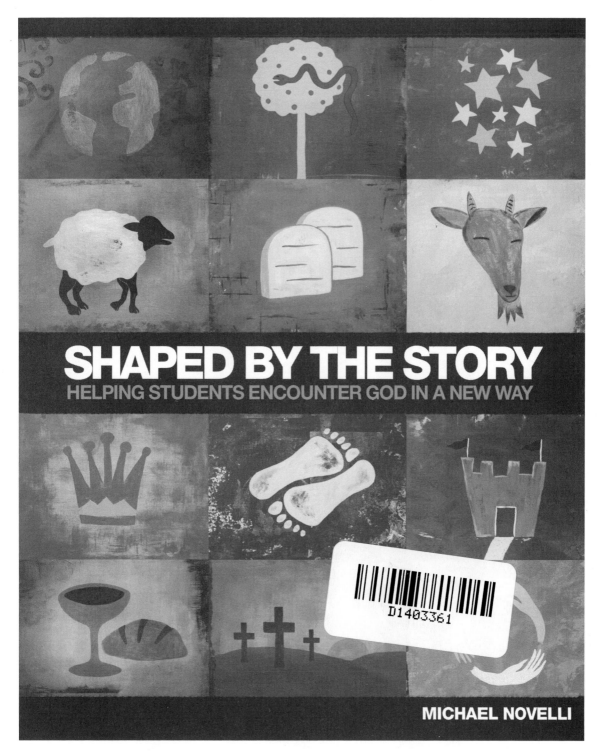

SHAPED BY THE STORY
HELPING STUDENTS ENCOUNTER GOD IN A NEW WAY

MICHAEL NOVELLI

 ZONDERVAN®

ZONDERVAN.com/
AUTHORTRACKER
follow your favorite authors

 youth
specialties

Shaped by the Story: Helping Students Encounter God in a New Way
Copyright 2008 by Michael Novelli

Youth Specialties resources, 300 S. Pierce St., El Cajon, CA 92020 are published by Zondervan, 5300 Patterson Ave. SE, Grand Rapids, MI 49530.

ISBN 978-0-310-27366-0

Cover and interior design by Mark Novelli, IMAGO MEDIA

Printed in the United States of America

08 09 10 11 12 • 20 19 18 17 16 15 14 13 12 11 10 9 8 7 6 5 4 3 2 1

DEDICATION

To my brother Mark who has walked with me through the entire storying journey over the last five years. Your continual encouragement and input have shaped this book and my life in immeasurable ways.

ACKNOWLEDGMENTS

Thanks to Michele, my brilliant and beautiful wife without whom I would be nothing. Also to my son, Angelo, without whose loving attention this book would have been finished in half the time!

To those who have walked with me and supported this dream since the beginning: Caesar Kalinowski, my partner in storying, whose faith and energy greatly inspire me; Jeff Frazier, my closest confidant who always tells me the truth; Kelly Dolan, whose energy and gifts help me to dream big; Seth McCoy, who challenges me in the best kind of ways; Phil Shields, who's shown great trust in me and anchored me with his wisdom; Kelli DeGroat, who continually offers help and encouragement when I need it most.

A great deal of gratitude is also owed to those who have encouraged me along the way: Amy Dolan, Josh Blair, Brandon Brown, Steve Argue, Dave Livermore, Josh Miller, Jen Howver, Mark Matlock, Jared Johnson, Jeff Vanderstelt, Andy Linquist, Tom Maxwell, Nate and Lisa Jarrot, Chris and Dawn Hansen, Aimee Novelli, and my parents—who ask me about my book every time I see them!

Thanks to all the youth workers, church leaders, and Merge staff who've trusted me enough to take on this grand experiment of engaging God's Story in a dangerous way!

I am so grateful for the efforts of Jay Howver to help me get this book published.

Much appreciation also to the rest of the folks at Youth Specialties—especially Mark Oestreicher, Tic Long, Dave Urbanski, and Roni Meek.

To the pioneers of Bible Storying who have blazed a trail ahead of me: John Witte, Grant Lovejoy, J.O. Terry—you are truly my heroes.

To the great Author and Creator...may your living story continue to shape us all.

CONTENTS

INTRODUCTION

Now more than ever, I'm amazed by the Bible.

Since I started following Jesus as a teenager, I've learned that the Bible is full of wisdom; I searched its pages for God's principles to live by. But I was always looking to surface the meaning behind the meaning—the pattern or the nugget that was applicable for my life. And I spent years studying and teaching the Bible this way.

Over the last several years, however, I've come to view the Bible in a different—and, I believe, more holistic—way. I now view the Bible as *a story.*

I love how stories have the power to take us on a journey. They show us new places and introduce us to new people. They draw us in, and we become a part of their adventures. And the best stories give us a glimpse of ourselves—they show us who we are and who we could be.

God's Story is like this. It stretches from the beginning of time, across our lives, and into the future. It tells of a great and faithful Creator who reveals the most beautiful way to live—in rhythms of love, peace, and sacrifice.

God, the great Author, continues to write this Story and desires us to find ourselves in it, discovering who we are and why we're here.

To be shaped by THE Story.

WHY I WROTE THIS BOOK

After 10 years in youth ministry, I felt as though I'd tried everything to help my students connect with the Bible. Then when a missionary named John Witte taught me the art of storying,

I realized it was more than just a new way to teach. It was a complete shift in how I could help students with their spiritual formation. It changed everything about the way I now look at my faith and ministry. (*Storying*, by way of definition, is a unique dialogue-centered approach to teaching the Bible. Guided by imaginative listening, creative retellings, and interactive discussions, storying inspires participants to find themselves in God's Story.) Storying made an impact on me—and the impact was big enough that it led me to spend the last several years helping others discover this amazing new (yet ancient) way of experiencing the Bible.

CLARIFICATIONS AND EXPECTATIONS

Throughout this book I'll use the words *narrative* and *story* interchangeably to describe a sequence of events that includes characters, dialogue, context, and plot. I'll also use the term *God's Story* to describe the entire collective story found in the Bible.

The Bible story helps us to see things from God's perspective—to reorganize our lives and priorities around God's ways. It challenges the ways and kingdoms of this world, and it also inspires us toward a better way—God's kingdom way.

I've discovered that the best way to let the Bible shape us is to experience it as story—to hear it, read it, and embrace it as a narrative. I regard the Bible as a living story—a true account that's illuminated and brought to life by the Spirit of God. This amazing story is intended to form our identity and give us direction as God's people. And this book is about how we might allow the Bible to form our lives and youth groups. That may sound simple but, as you probably know, life formation is a complex journey.

In order to take this journey with me, you must be open to—

- Interacting with the Bible in new ways
- Letting go of your expert status and becoming a colearner
- Expecting God to speak through his Story to and through each person
- Having fun, laughing, and enjoying learning
- Focusing on spiritual formation rather than behavior modification
- Sparking your students' imaginations and awakening them to what God has for them

What you *shouldn't* expect to get from this book—

- A formula for ministry success

- A trendy "postmodern" or "story" curriculum

- A foolproof method without possibility for failure and human error

- A process that leads to one conclusion or application from Scripture

- The only effective way to teach or learn the Bible

- A process that's easy to lead

This book is more of a starting point than a comprehensive guide. It marks where I am, and what I've learned over the past four years in my journey with storying. Even if you don't work with teenagers, I hope you'll benefit from the examples of my experiences with leading storying. I encourage you to step out, explore, let go, and try something new.

Bible storying is something better experienced than explained. In the back of the book is a DVD that takes you inside a real youth group as it experiences storying. Also included on the DVD is a Storying Promo Video and interviews. For more details about the DVD see the Appendix.

At the end of each chapter there are also questions to think about and discuss with your leaders.

For further resources, training, and ideas about storying, go to www.echothestory.com.

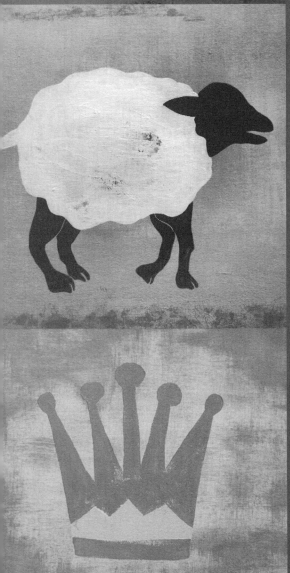

PART ONE
MY STORYING JOURNEY

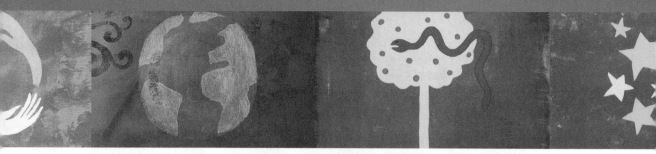

ADAGES AND PEP RALLIES
CHAPTER 1

My first memory of the Bible is from the stories we'd act out in Mrs. Mary's preschool class. I loved Mrs. Mary, and I loved going to preschool in the basement of the Methodist church in our small town. Mrs. Mary was such a nice teacher with a kind voice. She had short black hair, wore thick-rimmed glasses, and smiled a lot. She gave out lots of hugs and would often call us "sweetie" as she gently rubbed our backs. It felt like home most of the time—except for Bible story time. After a snack of juice and graham crackers, Mrs. Mary would gather us to the carpeted area for the Bible story. She opened a big trunk full of all kinds of hats, shirts, and props for us to use as we brought the day's Bible story to life. My brother and I called them "plays," and they were quite memorable. I wish I had video of them.

The most vivid story I remember us enacting was Jesus healing people with leprosy. My twin brother, Mark, and I (along with a few other students) were selected to play "sick" people in the story, while my friend Jeff was often picked to play Jesus. Not cool. (I believed it was because Jeff was the tallest kid in the class. But when I asked him why, Jeff said, "Because I live down the street." To my four-year-old mind that explanation made sense. Jeff must have had a special "connection" because he could walk to class. Maybe he came early and rehearsed his role as Jesus. Who knows?)

Worse yet, she asked us to put "leprosy spots" (made from purple clay) on our arms. Some of the kids were excited, but my brother and I wanted no part of this. In fact, we were freaked out, fearing these spots would morph into real ones and never come off. So when Mrs. Mary began the story, we both hid under a table, well out of the teacher's reach. We came out after a promise that no sores would be applied to our arms; but we still had to let Jesus heal us. A fair trade-off, I thought.

This memory had to, in some way, affect my view of the Bible. As a little kid, Bible stories seemed scary—storms, wars, sickness, spitting in people's eyes, blood, demons. No thanks.

We preferred Mom's stories about talking animals and magical forests over Mrs. Mary's Bible stories any day.

While I was growing up, the Bible seemed like an ancient history book to me, full of weird stories that I had no interest in reading. I remember spending one long Sunday afternoon watching Family Classics' presentation of *The Ten Commandments*. I was probably seven years old, and even then I could tell Charlton Heston's beard was a fake. And when he broke the two big "stone" tablets on the ground, I could tell they were obviously Styrofoam. *How lame!* I thought. "Come on, Mom. Can we turn on *Battlestar Galactica*?"

I did like the part when Moses parted the Red Sea and when he got electrocuted on the mountain. (Oh, wait a minute. I believe the lightning actually missed him. He still seemed pretty dumb for carrying around a big stick in a lightning storm.)

So my journey of faith was a path left mostly unexplored until I reached high school. Some friends invited my brother and me to a church youth group during my sophomore year. By then I had a genuine interest in spiritual things, but little understanding and few expectations. Youth group was a place where I quickly built friendships—and a good place to meet girls.

One day my youth leader, Dan, asked me, "Why do you read the Bible?"

"It makes me a better person...it's full of wisdom, right?" I asked.

"Yeah, but there should be more to it than that," he replied. This conversation occurred during the first year I'd ever picked up a Bible.

My spiritual interest eventually led me into some engaging conversations with a school friend named Maria. She was very bright and a practicing Catholic who was eager to investigate other paths of faith. So together we began learning about various religions. I even visited her church Mass, which was conducted mostly in Spanish. (What I liked most was her translating in my ear.)

When Dan found out that I was studying other religions, he showed me several Bible verses about the dangers of "false teachings." It scared me into ending my exploration. This memory makes me sad now, as I believe fear stifles learning. It's a distorted method for motivating people toward action.

Another time Dan told me that in order to grow spiritually I needed to have "devotions." This seemed odd to me: "Why do I need to read the Bible on my own if we're going to read it together?" Still, I began flipping around in the Bible aimlessly, like throwing darts at a board. After sifting through some of the books, I often landed in the books of Proverbs and James. These seemed the best places to find a quotation that would help me be a better person and live virtuously. At the time, I thought that religion was just about living morally, based on all religions as I understood them.

One night after youth group, Dan pulled me aside and started firing questions at me about why I came to church and why I read the Bible. At that time I'd just begun dating a girl from the youth group, and Dan said, "We don't let Christians date non-Christians." I wasn't sure what he was talking about. Was he talking about the girls I was friends with at school? I never thought of myself as a "non-Christian," and I'd never considered that there was an "us and them" thing going on. (Even now, I'm not sure this way of thinking is helpful.)

I told Dan, "I'm new to church. But I think people are at different levels with all of this… some of the healing stuff seems weird." He immediately showed me several verses about sin and separation from God, asking me if I understood that I was a sinner. "We all mess up," I replied.

Then he showed me a verse about how I needed to confess with my mouth and believe in my heart that Jesus is Lord. He asked me, "Who do you believe Jesus is?"

"I've always been taught that he's God's Son—"

"Do you really believe that in your heart?" he interrupted.

I paused; he stared at me. "Yeah…" I gulped. I was sweating, and I felt as though he was cross-examining me. I wanted Dan to like me. He was a good guy, fun to hang out with, and so genuine with us in the youth group. I was afraid I'd get kicked out if I doubted or had any questions. Yet I wasn't sure what it meant for Jesus to be "Lord."

Then Dan said, "You don't have to have all the answers to your questions; you have to have faith. If you really believe that, then say it out loud."

"Say what?" I asked.

"Jesus is Lord," he said.

I parroted, "Jesus is Lord."

Then he prayed for me. When we opened our eyes, he asked me, "Do you feel different?"

"I'm not sure," I answered.

"Well, you're changed now," Dan replied.

We talked some more. Dan told me the Bible is really about Jesus, and he encouraged me to read the Gospel of John. I went home and began reading that night. I was riveted by this story, and I read the Gospel all the way through in one sitting. Jesus was such a fascinating person and said such powerful things. I'd never seen him this way before. I was beginning to understand that God goes to amazing lengths in order to reach humans.

In the next few weeks, I read and reread John. Then I read the other Gospels. This was good stuff! It was one of the best stories I'd ever read—one I wanted others to know, too.

I told Dan what I'd been reading, and I asked him how I could help other people know about this story. He taught me to draw a diagram with Bible verses and simple steps to explain how to get to heaven. I asked, "Why not just have them read the story about Jesus?" One of the other youth leaders told me, "What if you have only a few minutes? People need more than the story; they need to know how to be saved."

This answer didn't satisfy me, but I wasn't sure why. It got me wondering why we needed the other parts of the Bible. We rarely talked about them in church, and I didn't see how they had much to do with Jesus. But my church insisted that the whole Bible is God's words. I was confused. The Old Testament was sometimes described in church as a "law book" that shows people how they can't live up to God's standards. That sounds depressing—why would I want to read that?

Thankfully, my doubts and questions didn't prevent me from pursuing God. The story of Jesus was so powerful that I decided to give my life to it. So I attended a small Bible college that was affiliated with my church, and I planned to study ministry as a vocation.

One of my pivotal classes was hermeneutics—how to interpret the Bible. This course taught us how to "exegete" passages of Scripture using a set of historical-critical skills. I was told that if I used these skills correctly—in tandem with the study of a passage in its original language—then I could arrive at the true meaning of the text. It was emphasized to me that there are "many applications to Scripture, but only one interpretation."

Then came a course in homiletics—how to prepare and preach a sermon. I was primarily taught the expository preaching method—a systematic way to teach a continuous segment of Scripture. This approach taught me to select a passage of Scripture, study it carefully, and try to surface the key points—usually three or four of them. Then I was to support each one of these points with related stories and Bible verses. To conclude, I was to tell my audience how to live out these concepts in their daily lives. This was the ministry one-two punch—historical-critical exegesis followed by expository preaching.

During my second year of college, I began leading a middle school ministry called "Discovery." This was my training ground in which to experiment with what I was learning. At the time, I was only 20 years old and new to Christianity. Therefore, I now equate this experience to letting your nine-year-old baby-sit your two-year-old—they might not burn your house down, but there will be a big mess when you get home.

Those are years of ministry that I wish I could do over. I consistently cared for students, yet my methodology was poor. But despite my mistakes, students from that youth ministry still tell me it was a positive and important group in their lives.

At first I tried expository preaching with these middle schoolers, but I gave up on it pretty quickly because the high school pastor didn't teach that way. He was more experienced than I was, and his topical style of teaching had his students in a frenzy for Jesus. Nevertheless, as time went on, I began to feel as though the church services and youth groups were just pep rallies for Jesus. And the main use of the Bible was to learn memory verses to ward off temptation. There was little room for doubts, struggles, or questions.

I felt out of place there. I wanted to be in a community where I could wrestle with my faith, be honest about my struggles, and explore a deeper understanding of the Bible and how to live authentically.

I spent the next few years attending larger congregations—some would say "megachurches." In some ways this was refreshing for my wife and me, as much of the teaching seemed to go deeper into the Bible and connect to real-life issues. But at the same time, we felt lonely. In the smaller church we came from, relationships seemed unavoidable. But in a megachurch, we had to work hard to connect with others.

I volunteered in a megachurch's high school group for two years. I had experience in running events and in creative arts, so I helped brainstorm and put together some of the weekly "programs" for the youth ministry. Excellence, cultural relevance, applicability, and authenticity were high values for our team. It was a fun group to serve with—they loved students and really desired to help them connect with God.

Our programs were mostly topical, focusing on life transformation and Christian living. I felt as though the content had depth to it, but it rarely focused on learning from the Bible. Instead, it emphasized ideas that are *supported* by the Bible. So we spent lots of time trying to determine what topics we should teach, usually picking the ideas we thought were the most relevant to students.

As I continued to serve this large group of students, I began to notice some interesting things. The big stage, professional lights and sound, and well-crafted programs and messages all created a different kind of youth ministry than I'd ever seen before. It seemed as though the majority of the students came to observe or evaluate rather than participate. They were audience members instead of members of a community.

Our creative team invested countless hours and creativity to put together programs that were engaging and interactive, but it was difficult to tell if what we planned made a difference.

A TRUE STORY ABOUT STORYING

I've rarely—if ever—seen students connect with and respond to Scripture the way they have through storying. Not only that, but also my own passion level and interest in God's Story has grown and deepened in ways that I never could've imagined.

Having led the storying process, it's been one of the absolute thrills of my life and work in ministry to watch students become enthralled with the Story of God, finding themselves completely caught up in (and a part of) the characters, patterns, and themes of the Bible.

I, like many others, had gotten to a point where I not only struggled each week to engage students in deep, meaningful dialogue about God and his ways, but I also found myself struggling daily to engage with God in my own life. It would be an overstatement to call storying the cure-all for both problems—but it sure feels close.

Having been a part of the storying process, both as a participant and a leader, I can truly say I'm unwilling to retreat to former, more familiar modes of learning and teaching the Bible. It's not that I find no merit in them. It's not that I won't try anything else. But I won't go back. I'm not sure I can go back.

Seeing (and teaching) the Bible as the Story of God and God's people throughout history (with today's church being the latest chapter of that story) has changed my life and ministry in unalterable ways.

—KELLY DOLAN, VOLUNTEER IN ARLINGTON HEIGHTS, ILLINOIS

Week after week, droves of students sat back in our theater-style chairs with their arms folded and offered little reaction.

Ironically, I also noticed that some of the students had a deep desire to be on the stage. Those teenagers in the band, drama, dance team, and especially those who helped with the teaching were revered as insiders—celebrities. I became concerned that we were feeding a culture that was already enamored with entertainment. And I worried that the students felt the same way my wife and I did—lonely and disconnected from real relationships.

Our environment and program seemed to influence the receptivity to our content so much that it made me believe Marshall McLuhan's adage, "The medium is the message."

I sensed that significant changes were needed in our ministry. But how? How could we help students connect with the Bible if our primary means of communicating with them was through a presentation on a stage?

QUESTIONS FOR RESPONSE AND DISCUSSION

What parts of this story do you relate to?

What Bible stories have most captivated you?

What have you been taught about why we read the Old Testament?

How do you read the Bible? In what ways have you changed the way you read it?

What kind of teaching do you best connect with?

How do you teach the Bible? How do you determine what you're going to teach?

How do the method and environment of our teaching affect the response of the learners?

EXPOSITION AND STAND-UP COMEDY
CHAPTER 2

How do I help make relationships central to ministry? How do I help students take ownership of their spiritual growth? What form does learning need to take to really connect?

These were the questions swirling in my mind from serving two years with programming at a megachurch. Right after that experience, I took a position as a high school pastor at a large congregation in the western suburbs of Chicago. The main thrust of this church's energy and resources was focused on Sunday services—of which an expository sermon was the centerpiece. These weren't elements that attracted me to the church, but it was the opportunity to lead a paid staff team for the first time and the freedom to shape a ministry that would hopefully help students live for God. Our goal was to center our ministry on relationships, Bible learning, and spiritual growth.

My style of teaching was laid-back. I strived to be practical and conversational, full of questions and stories. It wasn't long before church leadership strongly encouraged me to stick to expository teaching and stay in step with the church's philosophy.

Preparing expository messages was tough for me because I'm not very conceptual, but I'm very analytical. So when I'd try to examine, dissect, and draw out main points from a passage, I'd enter into a temporary paralysis: *What if I'm missing the "right" points? What if this stinks? Where can I find the perfect illustration to go with this?* It was common for me to anguish over each point of every message, trying to perfect it. And all the while, I'd be thinking in the back of my mind, *Why do I go through this every week? I bet there are still openings for me to go and work the drive-thru.*

Part of this was my neurosis (understandable) but not all of it. A portion of my discomfort with this approach came from feeling as though my *ideas* about the Bible, rather than the *actual* Bible, were center stage. I found that expository preaching often centers more on the main points that I choose to draw from the text, rather than the text itself. That means I could fit the Bible into my presentation, controlling it by the text I picked and how I supported each of my main points. I'd tell students what the passage said and then, as specifically as I could, share how they should live it out.

What was even scarier was how I found myself following some bad examples of expository teaching, saying things such as, "What Paul is saying here…" or "What Jesus is telling us is…," as if I'd uncovered what Paul and Jesus were REALLY trying to say. Yikes.

One thing that really bugged me as I taught was that it seemed as though my stories—supporting illustrations—were the only things the kids remembered.

I'm sure there are thousands of people more gifted at expository preaching than I. Perhaps there are many more who are also truer to the process. But my experience, after trying to teach this way for more than 10 years, is that this method is basically just an informed speech about Scripture—one person's educated opinion. That just didn't seem like enough for me or for my students. I wanted others to hear more of the *Author's* voice and not so much of mine.

One thing that really bugged me as I taught was that it seemed as though my stories—supporting illustrations—were the only things the kids remembered. I'd pour myself into a message, passionately share it, and the only thing students would say afterward was, "That story about when your friend pooped his pants at Six Flags was hilarious!"

Thanks, dude. Did you hear anything else?

I still have former students email me about some of the funny stories I told them years ago. I enjoyed making students laugh; in fact it was often a goal of mine. But it was never my primary goal. As time went on, I began to resent the idea that I was just a stand-up comedian to them. It seemed as though the students filtered out all of the other (more important) stuff I was saying and locked onto the humor. I guess I'd do the same thing, though.

In my second year of leading this youth ministry, the middle school pastor and I developed a plan to base our teaching topics on theology. We designed a teaching cycle for sixth through twelfth grades, covering 32 core Bible principles and virtues. Our plan seemed comprehensive and intentional. But man, was it complicated. It was like looking at the periodic table from chemistry class. I remember trying to explain this plan to parents and other staff members, and they all responded with glazed facial expressions. Their eyes said, "Good luck trying to pull that off!"

We felt as though we needed to be more intentional in helping students own their own faith. Researchers reported that between 50 to 70 percent of students active in youth ministries stop attending church in college—and the majority never return.[1]

My fear was that we were giving our students a brand of Christianity that was too simple and too shallow—irrelevant to the complexities of the life they would soon face in college. I was certain our teaching method was contributing to this; it felt as though all we were doing was digesting the Bible for our students and regurgitating it back to them in bite-size pieces, like a bird to its young.

I was determined to help students connect with God without always having to be the intermediary. I told our volunteers, "If the Bible is a living book that can change lives, then let's help students learn from it directly." We began meeting in house groups where a few small groups met under one roof with adult guidance. We moved these house groups to our primary meeting night each week and provided caring adults to reach out to every student who came.

One of our adult volunteers told me about a Bible study she was leading with girls from our youth group. She expressed how the approach she was using really helped get her girls into the Bible. I investigated this method further, and I liked it, too. This method seemed to direct people deeper into the text to search for the intended context and meaning. It was also simple enough that most anyone could do it. I was on board!

I spent a few months developing a training guide for our students. Then we spent a month training a core group of our students to lead these Bible studies with their peers. Adult coaches sat in on these small group sessions to make sure students focused on studying the Bible and kept on track theologically.

Two months into this process, we had some meetings to evaluate how this method was working in our groups. I got positive feedback from adult leaders who were amazed at how much the students wanted to learn. But only a handful of the student leaders were excited about how it was going.

Out of 20 student leaders, only seven felt as though their group connected with this method and really dug into the Bible. The majority complained it was like school—too much reading, thinking, and underlining—and their group was bored by it. A few students said it didn't apply to their lives—they wanted to talk about dating and real-life stuff. (I'm convinced there are a few students in every youth group who'd like us to teach about dating every week.)

As I asked for feedback in this meeting, students got into disagreements with each other. I felt like a referee—and I admit, I kind of enjoyed it. At least they were passionate about learning! A few student leaders drove the conversation and were adamant about our continuing to study the Bible this way. One student said, "The Bible is like our textbook for life. We need to study it like we would at school." I mostly agreed with him. My initial reaction was, "Suck it up. Being a Christian takes work. If you want to grow, then you have to study the Bible; it will pay off later." Then I added, "I'm not running a YMCA here." I regularly gave this reply when students complained about the group not being fun enough. (I'm pretty sure they hated my saying this.)

But the core question wouldn't go away: Why were more than two-thirds of my students struggling with this method? It wasn't laziness. They seemed to have the right motives— these were students who wanted to learn and to lead others. It made me wonder, *Is the Bible too cryptic for them to relate to on their own? Do we really have to tell them what it says?*

I observed each of our small groups in an attempt to uncover the real issues. And as I visited these groups, I noticed some interesting patterns.

First, a good majority of the students struggled with reading and comprehension. Many couldn't define simple words and struggled with reading aloud. This was especially surprising coming from upper-middle class families within highly rated school systems. Yet, basic literacy is essential to many Bible-study methods, so this was a big problem.

Second, students had very little Bible knowledge and background. How could this be? The vast majority of these students had grown up in our church. It didn't seem to matter what book of the Bible we picked to study, they didn't understand how it fit into the larger story. With only a few exceptions, students struggled to understand simple Bible terms such as *Jews*,

A TRUE STORY ABOUT STORYING

Storying isn't for the faint of heart. It's unpredictable. It's chaotic. It exposes what your students really believe. It takes effort. You can't control it, but you must be confident in it.

But for the brave, storying yields huge benefits. In the last year, my junior high students have wrestled with and talked their way through gnostic heresy. (They didn't name it as such, but that's what it was.) They've debated whether God is sexist because Jesus is a man and not a woman. They've connected the Old and New Testaments: No longer is the Old Testament about a "mean God" or the New Testament about a "teddy bear Jesus." They see a unified story—not a book with two main chapters. They can walk you through the main stories of Genesis from memory (most of which they hadn't heard before—or didn't remember hearing), even though we finished the patriarchs two months ago.

The senior highers love the process. They appreciate the respect of having their voices heard in a meaningful way, and when they spew out weird ideas, storying gives them a safe environment in which to explore their thoughts and learn to think theologically. At first I worried about what would happen if they came to the wrong conclusions or gave wrong answers. But it's been amazing to see communal correcting at work and to see how one or two questions will get them to bounce their thoughts off the story or the rest of the group. And they typically end up coming to the right answer without me having to tell them the right answer!

It's a process my youth leaders are excited about. Youth leaders who are mature, knowledgeable Christians and gifted teachers but had no interest in being a didactic Sunday school teacher have signed up to help out. Wheaton College professors and seventh graders build off each other's observations. One professor in particular looks forward to each week's story and what he'll learn.

Here are the three biggest benefits I've seen:

1. No matter how much or how little Bible knowledge a person has, everyone is placed on the same level.

2. Students learn to think theologically in a safe environment and to distinguish between things they've heard about God's Story and what's actually in God's Story.

3. Students see the Bible as one connected story to live out of and into.

One word of advice—if you decide to use storying, then you must go through the training. There's simply no substitute for experiencing it yourself before you lead others in it. You'll be surprised how much of an impact it has on you personally.

—JOSH MILLER, YOUTH WORKER IN GENEVA, ILLINOIS

gentiles, *the law,* idols, and so on. Even more of a concern was the fact that the majority of the students didn't believe it was important to understand the background of the passage.

Which led to my third observation: Discussions moved quickly to tangents and personal opinions. Little time was given to discover the author's intent. Most of what was shared were observations that students and adults heard in church and students' observations about the Bible. Then they'd tack on any meaning they wanted to, even if it had nothing to do with the passage. Context didn't seem important.

I was battling uphill against an ingrained approach to the Bible held by both our students and adults. I saw our groups skimming over the Bible like a self-help book, looking for bite-sized moral quips and handy life lessons. It seemed we'd learned to sift through the Bible while looking for a nugget of truth to extract, then ascribed our own meaning to it in order to apply it to our lives.

The Bible became just a conversation starter in our groups. I worried, *Maybe this is my fault. Maybe I didn't train them to follow the process correctly.*

When I asked Dean, one of the students I was mentoring, for his honest feedback, he said, "I'm having a hard time learning this way. It's so much reading—it feels like I'm trying to decode something. I'm really trying, but I feel like I just don't get it." Dean was one of my sharpest students.

I had no idea what to do. It seemed like we, and churches in general, were missing our students. I sensed a disconnect between the Bible and theology and students' lives. Honestly, I felt some of that same dissonance in my own life.

How could I help students embrace their own faith, learn, and grow? I know much of this responsibility rests on parents' shoulders, but I really wanted to make a lasting impact.

Changes were coming. The church leadership was becoming concerned that our ministry was too focused on small groups and not on a large program. They wanted someone who would lead the youth ministry primarily through teaching and upfront presence. I didn't fit this model they were moving toward, and I felt my opportunity for influence was shrinking fast, so I resigned.

Then, I really hit rock bottom. I started sniffing glue, and I lived in a dumpster. (Not really. I just wanted to see if you were still reading.) The story continues in the next chapter...

QUESTIONS FOR RESPONSE AND DISCUSSION

What parts of this chapter do you relate to? How?

What challenges have you faced in helping students engage with the Bible?

How do your students typically interact with the Bible?

Why do you think students might struggle with a literate, study-focused approach to learning the Bible?

What ways have you found that help students take ownership for their spiritual growth?

What kinds of Bible studies have you been a part of? In what ways were they helpful and not so helpful in studying the Bible?

NOTES

1. The Barna Group, "Twentysomethings Struggle to Find Their Place in Christian Churches," The Barna Update, September 24, 2003, http://www.barna.org/FlexPage.aspx?Page=BarnaUpdate&BarnaUpdateID=149 (accessed 3/30/08); LifeWay Staff, "LifeWay Research Uncovers Reasons 18 to 22 Year Olds Drop Out of Church," LifeWay Research, http://www.lifeway.com/lwc/article_main_page/0%2C1703%2CA%25253D1659 49%252526M%25253D200906%2C00.html? (accessed 3/30/08).

SPEAKING THE SAME LANGUAGE
CHAPTER 3

After leaving the big suburban church, my wife and I attended a small church in the same area. I volunteered to work with the youth group, and I soon found myself serving as the part-time youth director. I wasn't looking for a job, but this seemed to be a good fit for the church and for us.

For the first three or four months, I just observed the group and tried to build relationships with the students and volunteers. About 10 students attended the group each week; most were Christian-schooled or homeschooled. I'm not exactly sure how this played into the social dynamics of the group, but they showed little interest in each other. They'd often find the walls of the room and stay there. Needless to say, there was a lack of enthusiasm and energy in the group.

Many of the students' parents forced them to attend. After observing the group for a couple of months, I began leading the youth group programs. We immediately made some changes as we tried to build a sense of community and momentum. For instance, we began meeting in a home to create more of a family environment (this also helped us to include more volunteers with small children). We also played games to get students talking and having fun.

More students from the church began attending, but I think this was at the prompting of their parents who wanted to give me a chance. One of the students asked me, "So how long are you going to be here? We've had a different youth pastor every year for the past four years. I just want to know how long you plan on staying."

I wasn't sure how to answer this. I said, "I hope to be here a long time." He rolled his eyes a bit at my reply, and I began to understand why these students didn't engage: They hadn't had consistent leadership or relationships. This gave me a bit more compassion for these students and a little more patience for their apathy.

It was obvious to me that most of these students had a lot of prior exposure to Christian teaching and practices, and this familiarity caused some of them to see God as being commonplace and small. More than any other group I'd worked with, there was an underlying attitude that they knew it all.

About the same time I began working at this new church, my friend Caesar invited my brother, Mark, and me to a Chronological Bible Storying training session for missionaries at International Teams. I'd never heard of this method, but I trusted Caesar. We'd worked together at my former church, and we were becoming really good friends.

Caesar helped organize this training, and he invited a missionary named John Witte to lead it. Caesar had met John in an airport in Africa while doing some mission work.

John was a thin, Southern man in his late forties, with salt-and-pepper, crew-cut hair. He began the training by telling us how for more than 10 years he'd been teaching Bible stories to indigenous people in Africa, helping them to form an "oral Bible." I thought to myself, *An oral Bible? How can that be kept accurate?*

Many of the people John encountered had never even seen a written word, yet they learned deep truths about God through hearing and retelling Bible stories. The people of these tribes would sing songs and make up chants about the stories, and then they'd share the stories with other villages. John had seen how Chronological Bible Storying (CBS) was transforming lives among the tribes he worked with. He shared story after amazing story of how this approach to teaching was impacting people in Africa. (Read more of John's story in Appendix F.)

John found that leaving his Jeep behind, walking to different tribes, and living among the people was the most effective way of reaching them. By walking to the tribes instead of driving, John communicated his desire for equality, respect, humility, and patience to care for the people with whom he was sharing his stories. John would leave his Jeep and walk to tribes for six months at a time.

One of the stories John shared described an informal case study his denomination held comparing the Bible knowledge of oral learners to that of their literate seminary students. Through this study researchers discovered that the tribal people, who learned just from oral stories, showed as much—or more—depth of theology as those who learned from a seminary's systematic literary methods. After John told this story, I thought, *How could this be?*

I was fascinated by these stories, and they really challenged some of my assumptions about learning. After sharing the impact of storying, John led us through an experience with storying, something akin to what he did in Africa. He told more than 30 Bible stories, mostly from memory. These weren't loosely paraphrased stories, either, but accurate narratives with key dialogue—direct from the Bible. I was amazed at how much John had memorized, and I was even more amazed at how *captivated* we all were by these stories. And he told stories for more than three hours.

I have a hard time staying focused in most situations. (Maybe it has something to do with being raised in front of a television.) But these stories grabbed my attention and kept my interest like no sermon had ever done. It felt similar to watching a suspenseful movie or reading a novel in which the story unfurls right before you and all of the pieces fit together at the end.

In between most of the stories, John led us in a time of retelling and dialogue. By asking questions, he helped us discover connections and details about the characters that we'd never seen before. Theology was surfacing, and I was learning new things in a new way from stories I'd read dozens of times before and had thoroughly studied in college.

Most importantly, this was the first time I'd ever seen how the stories connected together so intricately and how the themes of God's restoration and kingdom way of life were woven through each story. It was profound. I knew many Bible stories, but I didn't know the Bible Story. I'd never seen the entire Bible as one great meta-narrative.

Like most of us, I was taught to look at only parts of the Bible, examining collections of true statements to study one by one and in small segments. Rarely did I hear the Bible told as story—and never like this. To be honest, I was a little disappointed that no one had ever shown me the Bible like this before. I wanted at least a partial refund on my college education (just kidding). Needless to say, this experience completely changed the way I teach and look at the Bible.

After the training, Caesar and I had dinner with John. He was so gracious, asking lots of questions about my family and me. As we talked, I got to hear more of his stories from the mission field and about his family. Caesar and I talked about our challenges with a "big" church and how we might remain relevant in a changing culture.

At one point in the conversation, John asked me directly, "You seem really excited about this method. How do you plan to use it?"

I stumbled over my words, finally saying, "I'm not sure. I'd like to try this with my youth group, but I'm concerned because I'm sure they've heard these stories a million times."

John replied, "You have, too, right? How did you respond?" (He was doing that Jedi mind thing he's so good at—helping me find my own answers.)

"Yeah. You're right. I need to help them come to the stories in a new way."

Then John said, "God's Story is living. If we really trust that, then we'll listen to it and learn from it our whole lives. Not too many people are trying storying here in North America. You need to think bigger than your church. People need this here,

> **Meta-narrative:**
> A grand, overarching, all-encompassing story that gives meaning and order to life—past, present, and future.

especially teenagers. You're the right ones to figure this out." John was convinced the story approach would work well in American culture already captivated by stories, as statistics were showing that more people were choosing to learn through nonliterate means.

Caesar and I looked at each other, not knowing how to respond. I was scared. I thought, *I can barely memorize my phone number—how can I do this? How can I help people all over the country when I'm not sure I can help the students in my youth group?*

Caesar answered, "You're right, John. We want to start trying this out. Can you show us some of your stories to help get us started?"

John said, "Sure, but I'll have to write them down. I've been meaning to do that anyway."

I thought, *What a freak—he doesn't even have them written down. Oh yeah...this is going to be real easy.*

I nervously asked, "How important is it that we memorize the stories?"

John said, "I think it's the best way to do it. It's critical that the stories become a part of who you are...and that takes time. Be patient. You'll figure it out. God will help you just like he helped me."

I knew he was right. I'm impatient, and I'd switched to logistics mode already. Even though I was intimidated by the task of figuring this out, I felt as though something supernatural had happened during our conversation. The best way I can describe it is that it felt as though God were speaking through John to us—calling Caesar and me to help people know God through God's Story. There was no turning back.

I still wasn't sure how my home schoolers and Christian schoolers would respond to Bible stories, but I was willing to try it. Soon after the training, I put together a night where we told the stories of the lost coin, the lost sheep, and the lost son. I didn't teach about them or give background information—we just let the stories speak. I worked with two of my adult volunteers to help them tell the stories as *stories*, instead of just reading them.

Before we began, I told the students to listen to the stories as though they'd never heard them before—and really concentrate. Afterward, we broke up into our gender-specific small groups for discussion. I let volunteers lead the discussions using questions I'd written based on the Bible storying method. The questions guided us toward observation, asking: *What did you notice for the first time in the story? What did you learn about God? What did you learn about humans?* and so on.

As soon as the discussion started, I noticed a different tone in our group than I'd seen before. They seemed *interested* in sharing and listening to each other. That night, we had the deepest and most engaging discussion about the Bible that I'd ever encountered with students. They actually *wanted* to talk about the Bible.

It seemed as though the story was a key that unlocked something for us—like we were now all speaking the same language. For the first time, students wanted to keep talking about the stories until after it was time to go home. Parents were waiting at the door.

After the students left that evening, I had our regular feedback meeting with the adult volunteers. My wife and the other female leaders shared similar responses from their students:

A TRUE STORY ABOUT STORYING

Storying is actually one of my favorite things to do. I get really excited when God speaks to me through other people. I love the sense of mission that comes when we talk in community about God's Story and what God is like. The characters in the Bible have become more human and earthy since we started going through the stories. There are actually, literally, three dimensions to God's Story and to all its characters. All the stories in the Bible happened on the same planet we're on right now. And each little piece (such as the story of Joseph or the story of God's covenant with Abraham) doesn't stand on its own. It's part of a greater tale. God is so big—and God's Story can be known only through a saga. And no single picture describes God, either. The only way humans can attempt to illustrate God is through a story that spans the whole history of the earth.

Through the stories, I'm realizing that God actually wants ME and the life I'M living to become a part of restoring his garden of Eden dream for the world. I don't know if there's anything more beautiful than a God who dreams of peace and wholeness to come to all creation.

For me, the story of the Bible reveals God's dream for the world. Knowing the story of God's interaction with human beings allows me to find my place in the activity of God's kingdom. As his church, we can begin working toward realizing God's dream for all people. Knowing the story helps me know how to continue that story. Seeing what God has been working to accomplish in human history allows me to take my place in this plan of restoration.

By realizing that God's dream is for humanity to be united and connected, sharing our lives and resources with one another, I can give myself to making that happen in my life. The kingdom of God won't be a destination only in the future; it can be a present reality that grows through the healing of our broken souls as we come to find life in our Creator.

Through the Story I'm realizing that inner transformation propels God's kingdom. As we see God's Story come to life, and as we begin to see our world with God's eyes, we can be changed on the inside and then bring change to the people and places we find around us. God's Story shows us God's heart for all creation, and we see the wholeness and love God has for human beings.

And as humans who are being made whole, we can work toward God's dream that the world will be more beautiful, and that we'll restore it, connecting our hearts with God's to bring *shalom*—peace and wholeness—to the whole world.

—NATALIE POTTS, HIGH SCHOOL STUDENT IN EAST ST. PAUL, MINNESOTA

"The girls wouldn't stop talking and giving input. This is the first time that's happened." "This really got them thinking about the story; usually they just talk about their own problems."

This was in the spring, but I wanted to figure out a way to experiment with this method of teaching throughout the upcoming school year. With Caesar's help I immediately started working on narratives. I viewed the stories we were stitching together as a bridge that would lead people back to the Bible and get them excited about the greatest story ever told.

I started with 12 stories, but we felt compelled to expand this into a set of 21 stories from Genesis to Acts 2. I used some of John Witte's outline to guide us in choosing which stories to tell. The goal was to put together a set of stories that would paint a picture of God's restorative plan—Caesar called it "a redemptive arc." I aimed to remain true to the biblical texts, preserving key events and dialogue. I did my best not to embellish with my own exposition, addition, elaboration, or cultural perspectives. I wasn't trying to "modernize" the stories; I just wanted to tell them chronologically and accurately.

I spent months comparing English translations as I put together each narrative, largely basing the content on the New International Version and New Living Translation. In certain spots, key ideas were emphasized or repeated to draw out a character's qualities. These narratives are still a work in progress.

It was a worthy investment that initially took me more than 1,200 hours over a 16-month period. (By the way, you can download these narratives for free at www.echothestory.com.)

By the fall I was close to halfway finished with the first attempt at stitching together narratives. In any regard, I was far enough along to begin telling these stories with my group. The experiment had begun.

QUESTIONS FOR RESPONSE AND DISCUSSION

Which parts of this chapter did you relate to your own story?

How do students in your group view the Bible?

Why do you believe people connect with stories?

How have you incorporated storytelling in your ministry?

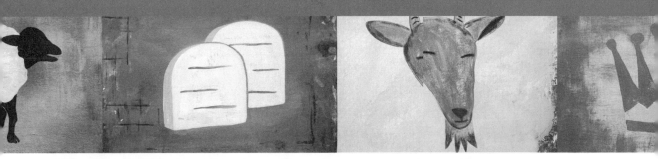

THE STORYING EXPERIMENT
CHAPTER 4

At the beginning of the next school year, I began a nine-month process of telling, retelling, and discussing stories with my youth group. I was a little surprised at first when the students didn't know how to react to them (since they seemed so excited by the initial trial runs). As we went through the first two stories, they asked questions such as, "So when are you going to teach us?" "Why aren't we studying the Bible?" "Why don't you tell us how to apply this story?" and "What does this have to do with everyday life?" And I'd usually respond, "Be patient with this; we're going to try something new. We're not getting rid of our Bibles. In fact, I think this will get you *more* interested in reading them. You'll soon see how this matters in your life." I felt as though we were going through a detox program together— trying to strip off all the layers of expectations regarding how we're supposed to come to the Bible. It required a lot of patience, grace, and consistent yet gentle reminders of why we were doing what we were doing.

The first few weeks were challenging. I could see the "we've heard this story a million times" look in their eyes. But then, when we got to the story of Cain and Abel, something changed. It was the same reaction I'd had when John Witte told the stories. When we got about three or four stories into the process, the students began to see how the stories are interrelated. They shared all kinds of connections between the creation story, the separation story, and Cain and Abel. I envisioned imaginary light bulbs turning on above their heads.

Now the students' excitement about the stories was building. I could tell because their level of engagement was so much higher; they wanted to retell the stories and to offer their observations—without being asked. They were becoming fully engaged. Things weren't perfect, though. There were still distractions, and some students disengaged at times; but overall, we were becoming a different group—a community forming around God's Story.

Each week, after our hangout and mealtime, we'd review the previous stories we'd covered. I tried to make this creative and fun, using art, drama, music, and so on. The reenactments of the stories were always the most enjoyable—and surprisingly pretty accurate. We used symbols for each story to help us connect with something visual. Reviewing the stories also helped any new people get up to speed on what we'd already covered.

After the review, I'd give my pep talk to set the tone for the story. I called it getting in "listening" mode. I'd say something like this:

> Right now we're going to try a new approach to learning from the Bible called "storying." This approach is rooted in the ancient Hebrew way of learning through observation and dialogue.
>
> The Hebrew people had a unique way of looking at the Scriptures…they called it "The 70 Faces of Torah"—the Torah being the first five books of the Bible.
>
> They got this phrase by comparing the Scriptures to a beautiful diamond with 70 sides—or faces. Hearing and studying the Scriptures was likened to holding up and turning that diamond—allowing the light to reflect further beauty, depth, detail, and brilliance.
>
> Just like the ancient Hebrews, we believe that the Bible and its stories are living and have meaning and mystery that we can discover today.
>
> We must choose now to turn the diamond, looking for more that's within the story. We do this expecting God to illuminate something new to each one of us.
>
> When you see something in the story—something simple or beautiful or profound—you need to share it with the group! That's how we learn through storying—we listen to all the different reflections from God's Story. Each one is important and can teach us something new.
>
> This process isn't easy. It takes concentration and something called "imaginative listening." What do you think it means to be an imaginative listener?
>
> *Imaginative listening* means using your imagination to picture the story in your mind like you would a movie, where you're actually *in* the scene.

After we're done listening to this story, we'll retell it as a group. Pay attention to the details of the story because I will ask you about them!

If it helps you to concentrate, close your eyes during the story or write down your thoughts, or choose a focal point to look at in the room.

Are you ready? Take a moment in silence to slow down and clear your mind. Now whisper a prayer asking God to speak to you through this story.

This introduction to the story really helped our group get into the right frame of mind. I used some variation of this talk every week because the storying process is very repetitive and I knew some of my students who are used to experiencing constant change through media and video games might lose focus. I had to be mindful of this tendency and continually coach them to be attentive. I reminded them, "We need each of you to share with us as one through whom God is speaking. You're the teachers."

I'd also remind them, "You don't come to these stories as children or even as you did just a year ago. You're growing into adults, and God is expanding your mind and desiring to show you new things. These stories aren't the entire picture of God's plan. It's kind of like we're gazing out of a skylight—we see just a glimpse of the expansive sky overhead. This story is just a glimpse of how big and how awesome God is. As God shows you new things, he desires for you to show them to us so we can see more of who God is as well."

I realized early in the process that my job was more of a guide than an instructor, leading our group on the journey into God's Story. We'd learn and explore together, and I'd help frame our experiences and keep us on the path. Most of the time I felt as though I was learning more than the students were learning.

The storytelling time was never more than 10 minutes long, and I really worked at trying to bring the story to life with words, rather than just reading it. We also kept it low-tech. I never used music, visuals, or video. (Sometimes I'd light a candle to symbolize the beginning of the listening mode.) This isn't to say those tools can't help, but I was concerned that in such a small group they'd become more of a distraction than a vehicle toward building imagination and listening.

By now our group had grown from about 10 to 18 students, and we met all together for most of the youth group time. We'd sit in a circle in one of our students' living rooms; and after the storytelling, we'd do a quick group retelling to recount the events of the story. I led this time by asking questions such as, "What happened first in the story? What happened after that?" Though simple, it was very beneficial in building the students' retention.

As we reviewed and retold the stories, something very interesting began to happen—something I call "communal correcting." The group began to work together and help each other remember key details. When someone missed something or said something inaccurate, the group would correct him or her—usually in a gentle way. This was better than my stepping in as "the expert" and setting things straight.

Following the retelling, we stayed together as an entire youth group for story dialogue. I'd usually begin this time by setting up some ground rules: Everyone is expected to participate, your observations matter, this isn't about offering the "right" answers, and no jumping ahead to future stories—only connect the current story to ones we've already covered in the chronology.

The first questions I'd ask were "wondering" types of questions, such as, "What did you notice for the first time in this story?" "What did you picture in your mind as the story was being told?" and "What does this story make you wonder about?" This really helped disarm the students, and it allowed them to use their imaginations. When students asked questions about the story out of wonder (for instance, "Who was Cain afraid would attack him if he and his family were the first humans?"), I wouldn't give my opinion or an expert's answer; I'd just affirm them, saying, "That's a great question. I wonder about that, too" or "Would someone be willing to research that a bit this week and share what you learn the next time we meet?"

This took my students some getting used to because they expected me, the Bible teacher, to give them all the answers. But by allowing this kind of wondering and tension, we provided space for the stories to become real events in our minds. The stories became bigger than just allegories and fairy tales because we began looking at them from a different perspective.

After our dialogue time, we broke into gender-specific small groups—usually one guys' group and two girls' groups. Chris, my intern, led the guys' group most of the time, and I observed. We sometimes called these "my story groups," as the focus was on sharing ways we saw our own stories connecting with God's Story and with each other. We focused these times on praying, caring for each other, and sharing how we saw God shaping us. We never told the students how to apply the stories, but we did ask some pointed questions, such as, "How does this story challenge or encourage you to live?" These times were filled with honesty and amazing insights from our students.

Toward the beginning of the year, we took turns sharing our personal stories within these groups. One of the new guys in our group began sharing his story. He was a small, quiet sophomore, and we really didn't know much about him. Still, he opened up about his life, and he shared how he'd brought his mom to our church and it had changed their lives. Then he said something I'll never forget: "I'm learning more than ever before. I saw that I really wasn't a believer. The stories pulled me back in." He broke down and began crying, which led to a long, awkward silence. Then, spontaneously, the other guys got up and embraced him, and many of them started crying, too. These were guys who wouldn't even say hello to each other just months earlier, and now they were embracing in a giant group hug. Wow! The other volunteers and I just sat there in awe. God was doing something significant in us, and God's Story was right in the middle of it all.

Each week I gave out cards with the Scripture for that week's story. Without my prompting, students were coming back the next week with observations and questions after reading more about the story. The story sparked a desire to learn more and to actually read the Bible. A few students told me they studied the stories as part of their daily devotional time. And one student sarcastically asked me in front of the rest of the group, "Why didn't you tell us Noah got drunk and naked at the end of the story?" Even though this wasn't a funny part of the story, our whole group burst out laughing.

> **The stories became bigger than just allegories and fairy tales because we began looking at them from a different perspective.**

We took a month off over Christmas break. When we resumed in January, we did a review of all the stories from the fall. My friend Caesar was visiting from out of town, so he got his first glimpse at how the stories were impacting my group. However, on the way to youth group that night, I tried to downplay what was happening for fear the students wouldn't remember much about our stories after the break. "We'll see what happens," I said in a skeptical voice. "I'm not sure how this review will go tonight."

At the beginning of our time together, I handed out cards with our symbols for each story written on them, and I asked the students to pair up and put the stories in order. We'd gone through about 10 stories so far, and I assumed they'd struggle to remember some of them.

The students worked together with only a few disagreements, and they had all of the stories mostly in the right order. I think I had to switch only two people around. So far, so good.

Then I asked the students to tell us what they knew about the stories on their cards. So beginning at creation, we went down the line, and some students told the stories word for word. Caesar and I looked at each other in amazement. Jacob and Esau, the exodus, the tabernacle—these are stories with lots of details, and the students were retelling most of them. I was so encouraged to see them excited about God's Story, I was in tears.

One student asked, "What's wrong, Mike?"

"Don't you see?" I said. "God's Story is capturing each of you. It's becoming a part of your stories."

"Yeah, this is pretty cool," another student replied.

It wasn't about memorization; it was about students being excited about how the Bible could change their lives.

One student shared, "These stories are giving me a picture of how I should and shouldn't live. I can relate to the struggles of the Israelites...it makes me see how much I need God."

Momentum was building now, and students began inviting their friends to our group. One of the girls said, "I wasn't too sure about this idea at first, and I didn't really want to invite my friends to come and hear old Bible stories. But once we got into it, it was way better than I expected. And my friends really wanted to come and learn." This was a girl who seemed disengaged most of the time, but she became a magnet for bringing unchurched friends to our group.

I also noticed that a volunteer's wife was now coming every week. She was so involved in the kids' ministry and music ministry at the church that I knew she didn't really have time to come to youth group. But she said to me, "I've taught these Bible stories for years, but this is new and different. I want to come every week to find out what's going to happen next in the story and to see the 'light bulbs' go on."

"Well," I teased, "you *can* read ahead..."

We saw these students become transformed by God's Story. Do you know how I could tell change was happening? The questions, observations, and connections they were making went deeper and deeper each week.

A TRUE STORY ABOUT STORYING

When I was introduced to the storying process, I had a lot of reservations and wondered how in the world my students would connect with it. I wondered if I was doing the Scripture a disservice or throwing it out all together by storying. Yet for some reason my curiosity dug deeper into storying and its ability to connect students to God's Word.

We did a summer trip two years in a row to an event called Merge—a weeklong high school gathering during which students dig into God's Story in deeper ways through creative storytelling, art and media, discussion groups, learning stations, and interactive experiences. The entire week centered on storying and seeing how we fit into the Story of God. As I watched and helped facilitate discussion with my students, I saw the story unfold and students connect to the Bible unlike anything I'd seen before. I saw them discuss and question things to take them further into who God is and who they are in God's Story. It was amazing watching the light go on in so many minds and then pushing them to dig further into the Bible on their own.

What hit me afterward was how many of my students had never experienced this sort of learning and dealing with the stories of the Bible. So the next step was to bring this method to our entire group and see what happened.

This was a difficult transition, but it was one I was curious about. And since none of our underclassmen had experienced this, we introduced it for seven nights and geared everything around the story. Then discussion groups, led by our adult leaders, dove deeper into the scenes to see what each person could learn from the next. This meant our leaders didn't teach; they were learners right alongside the students.

What we heard next was interesting. Students were saying things such as, "I've never heard this story before, and I loved it." My thought was, *How is that possible when they're talking about the story of Moses?* Yet this is what was taking place. The students who were new to this were intrigued and listened intently; older students continued to dive deeper; and we all journeyed together. This impacted not only our students and leaders, but also me.

As I worked through this process, I found myself dealing with the Bible in creative ways, and I read it with more of an awareness of things I'd always missed before. I asked questions about what was taking place. And even though most of those questions never got answered, it still drove me further into the Word and connecting with it. This process forced me into interaction with my Creator and made this guy who grew up with the Word of God see it again for the first time.

That's what's so necessary for us today: To start cherishing the story of the Bible as though it's the first time we've ever heard it. When we get back to that level of appreciation, the story becomes real again—instead of being something we take for granted. This approach to Bible study will continue to be a part of our lives with students. After all, when students are glued to stories—life-giving stories—what more could we ask for?

—PHIL SHIELDS, YOUTH WORKER IN MACKINAW, ILLINOIS

One of the guys shared with our small group, "I find myself telling these stories to some of my friends at school—and some of them don't know God at all. It's also inspiring me to write songs about God." For several weeks he came back with stories about how his friends were interested and asking questions about the stories at the lunch table.

During her first visit, one girl shared, "I've never heard these stories before; they're really interesting." A few weeks later, she opened up to the girls' small group, telling them, "Tonight, I realized that the stories you're telling are going a different direction than my own life. How can my life be a part of what you're doing?" The girls and adult leaders encouraged her and prayed for her and drew her into their community. This was an amazing moment. We hadn't gotten to the story of Jesus yet, and this girl recognized that God's Story calls us to be a distinct people and knew she wanted to be a part of that.

 Around Easter we held a Seder with our students. (A Seder is a symbolic Jewish meal that's held during the annual Passover celebration in remembrance of how God rescued the Hebrews from their slavery in Egypt.) This was our second year of hosting a Seder for students, but this one was different. The experience seemed much richer because we were already immersed in the story.

We prepared an elaborate Jewish-style meal for the students, complete with many traditional Passover items. The word *Seder* means "order," so we followed a *Haggadah*—which means "explaining"—a booklet I developed filled with prayers, readings, and points of interaction. We began the Seder with the exodus story and concluded with the Last Supper story.

This celebration came alive right in front of us, giving powerful new meaning to the symbols, imagery, and rituals of the exodus. It also helped us connect the stories of Abraham's covenant and the new covenant in Jesus, giving us a deeper understanding of Jesus as the true Messiah. All of us who took part in this Seder were deeply moved by it, and it continued to be one of the most powerful moments I've ever experienced in youth ministry.

"Aren't we supposed to be God's blessing to others like Abraham was?" one student asked. "Well, my brother and I have a couple of ideas about this..." This student initiated opportunities for our group to regularly serve meals to the homeless, and he led an outreach for students at his school. He did all of this because he saw himself as a continuation of God's Story—to be God's blessing to the world. I was really encouraged when this same student decided to change his college plans so he could pursue youth ministry.

A few weeks later we came to the story of Jesus' death and resurrection. I was concerned that students were too familiar with this story. *The Passion of the Christ* had just been released in theaters, and our church had gone to see it together. I wondered if it was too much for the students to process. But I was wrong. The story gave us another entry point to reflect on the sacrifice of Jesus. Students related the details of this story back to the tabernacle, the Passover, and the words of the prophets. There were nonstop connections taking place, adding even more meaning and depth to our times together. One student said, "It's amazing how at the end you realize how all of the stories connect—they all point directly to Jesus."

Instead of going to our small groups, the students initiated an impromptu prayer time. For 30 minutes they prayed out loud, giving thanks, crying, and expressing their hearts to God for the life of Jesus given in place of their own. They were simply responding to the story—their story.

Two weeks later we had a celebration to finish the school year. We grilled and had a lot of fun playing games outside. The students' parents came that night, too. The highlight for me was a sharing time during which the students shared how the Story had shaped their lives over the past year.

Here are just a few of the responses from these students:

> "The stories challenged me to look beneath the surface and search for more about God's character. I learned something new from every single story."

> "I saw these stories in a new light. I want to read them over and over again!"

> "I (now) see that the Bible isn't boring but full of amazing info. And stories that can impact my life."

> "I couldn't stop thinking about the stories. Some of the questions were so difficult that they made me want to go and search for the answers."

> "The stories changed my whole perspective on my faith. They made me want to live for God because God is amazing—and those stories prove it."

> "The stories and discussion really challenged the way I viewed the Bible and the perspective I've had about Christianity. It really helped me dig deep and actually understand the story. I'm now challenged to live [my life while remaining] open to whatever Jesus calls [me to do]."

Toward the end of our youth group time, one of the parents pulled me aside. "I need to talk to you," she said. I was a bit concerned, as she was a protective homeschooling mom who was also very vocal. I worried I'd done something wrong. Then she said, "My son has been learning about the Bible in homeschool his entire life. But this year has been amazing. He's learned more from these stories about God than from anywhere else."

I replied, "Thank you, that's so kind of you to say. I'm not sure that's really true, though. I believe that all of your investment in his learning now has a context. These stories have helped your son develop a mental timeline so he can see and understand all that you've taught him from a broader perspective."

For many of my students, it seemed as though God was no longer small and common-place in their minds. God was revealing himself to them through his Story. I saw God shaping and forming students right in front of me. They got a glimpse of a God who's not only bigger than they ever imagined, but also more loving, more mysterious, more unpredictable, more just, and more personal.

I say all this not to point to something I did, but to point to God and his Story, which is still living and active and can capture the hearts and minds of all of us. This experience trans-formed not only my group, but it also changed me. I was shaped by the Story.

If we come to the Bible as a story, as I believe God intended for us to do, then it takes on a form that can be experienced. In this experience of God's Story, God gives us a picture of who we're created to be, and God calls us to join in his activity around the world.

QUESTIONS FOR RESPONSE AND DISCUSSION

Which parts of this chapter did you relate to your own story?

What are the similarities and differences between storying and your current teaching methods?

In order to be effective, what do you believe storying requires from the leader? From the student?

How would your students respond to storying? What challenges do you believe you'd face? How might it help them to learn?

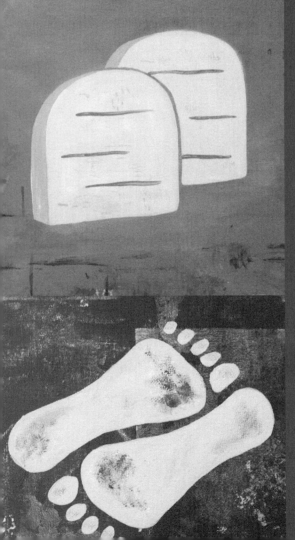

PART TWO
THE WHYS AND HOWS OF STORYING

COMMUNICATION REVOLUTION
CHAPTER 5

A shift has taken place in America over the last few decades. The source of learning and information is no longer centered on printed words, but on visual and auditory media. While many learners in our part of the world still have a base of literacy, it seems we mostly rely on reading when it's necessary for accessing media.

Over the last 15 years, what changes have you noticed in the way people learn and communicate? How about in the last five years?

STATISTICS ON LITERACY AND MEDIA

People have different opinions on the use of statistics. Some feel they give valuable insights, while others think they're just unsubstantiated spin. Whatever your take, I believe that looking at data will provide us with some indicators on how people are gathering information in our society. Without a doubt, our access to digital media and the Internet has influenced the way we learn.

The following are some statistics I've gathered from a variety of sources.

LITERACY

The 2003 National Assessment of Adult Literacy (NAAL) is the nation's most comprehensive measure of adult literacy. About 19,000 adults participated in the national and state-level assessments, representing the entire population of U.S. adults age 16 and older, who speak English or Spanish, and don't suffer from mental disabilities. This report found that:

- As many as 46 million adults in the U.S. are below the basic level of literacy. That means they have difficulty reading even the simplest written materials. (For example, they'd have trouble locating an intersection on a map, understanding a prescription, or following directions in a cookbook.)[1]

- As many as 70 million of adults in the U.S. are at the basic level of literacy. This means they struggle to comprehend and process detailed written materials. (For example, they'd have trouble summarizing information they've read and locating and using information on forms such as job applications, maps, and graphs.)[1]

- Assessments of this report indicate that 50 percent or more of Americans are at or below basic literacy levels. People in this category are described as having "low literacy"—or being functionally illiterate—having reading and writing skills insufficient for ordinary practical needs.[2]

- 58 percent of the U.S. adult population never reads another book after high school.[3]

- 42 percent of college graduates never read another book.[3]

- 57 percent of new books aren't read to completion.[3]

- Most readers don't get past page 18 in a book they've purchased.[3]

- A poll of fifth graders' reading habits outside of school revealed that 50 percent read four minutes a day or less outside of school, 30 percent read two minutes a day or less, 10 percent read nothing.[4]

- 80 percent of graduating high school seniors say they'll never again voluntarily read a book.[5]

- 65 percent of college freshmen read for pleasure for less than one hour a week or not at all.[6]

- 70 percent of Americans haven't visited a bookstore in five years.[3]

- A 2006 study shows that the time kids spend reading for fun declines sharply after age eight and continues to drop off through the teenage years.[7]

- More than 20 percent of adults read at or below a fifth-grade level—far below the level needed to earn a living wage.[8]

- Half of U.S. households didn't purchase a book in 2001.[3]

- Customers 55 and older account for more than one-third of all books bought in 2001.[3]

- Between 1996 and 2001, people reduced their time spent reading to 2.1 hours a month.[3]

- At least 1.5 billion people in the world have never been introduced to reading and writing.[9]

MEDIA STATISTICS FOR THE UNITED STATES

- In 2006, the average American home had more television sets (2.73) than people (2.55). More than 50 percent of homes have at least three working televisions.[10]

- On average, televisions are turned on for eight hours and 14 minutes a day.[10]

- The average adult watches four hours and 35 minutes of television each day. Kids average about four hours a day.[10]

- Children who have televisions in their bedrooms: 32 percent of two- to seven-year-olds and 65 percent of eight- to 18-year-olds.[11]

- 35 percent of children and teenagers have video game systems in their rooms.[12]

- 72 percent of kids ages eight to 17 years old report multitasking while watching TV.[12]

- Children average 6.5 hours a day—more than 44 hours a week—in front of a screen (TV, computer, video game, and so on).[11]

- 35 percent of "tweens," defined as kids ages eight to 12, own a mobile phone; 20 percent use text messaging; and 64 percent download and play music on their phones.[13]

- 12- to 17-year-olds average 26.6 minutes each day instant messaging (IM).[14]

- More than 70 percent of Americans ages 15 to 34 use social networks online.[15]

- Nearly two-thirds of teenagers—63 percent—have a cell phone.[16]

- 87 percent of those aged 12 to 17 use the Internet—that's about 21 million preteens and teenagers.[17]

- Teenagers average 16.7 hours and adults average 11.6 hours of weekly Internet usage.[14]

- Americans aged 13 to 18 spend more than 72 hours a week using electronic media—defined as the Internet, cell phones, television, music, and video games. Because teenagers are known for multitasking, their usage of devices can overlap.[18]

- 68 percent of teenagers have created profiles on social networks such as MySpace, Xanga, or Facebook.[18]

What's your reaction to those statistics? How do you think technology is influencing our culture in North America?

THE DIGITAL ERA

Steve Jobs, founder of Apple Computer and creator of the iPod, was recently asked what he thought of the Kindle, Amazon's new digital book reader. Jobs replied, "It doesn't matter how good or bad the product is, the fact is that people don't read anymore...Forty percent of the people in the U.S. read one book or less [in 2007]."[19]

Even if these statistics offer only part of the picture, it's easy to see signs every day that communication has changed. It seems most Americans spend their nonworking time in front of a screen. Every place you go, someone is texting or talking on a cell phone, and digital music players and video displays are everywhere.

When I get home from work, I can watch virtually any movie or television program, shop, research, learn new things, or play any game I'd like, accessing them through the Internet, game console, or a digital video recorder. I enjoy and benefit from continuous access to media, but it's definitely a distraction. And I'm sure I read and interact face to face with people less often because of this.

With the constant lure of technology, it's not hard to see how people are drifting away from reading books. Books almost seem out of place in this high-tech world. And I've noticed that it takes more discipline for me to read now than it did just five years ago. I have to slow down and get into a certain frame of mind to read, especially to read for enjoyment. Most of my current reading tends to be a means to an end—I'm trying to dig for information. Unfortunately, that's the way I read the Bible for many years, too.

I once said during a storying training session that "the Internet and text messaging are not literate means of communication...they're more visual than literate...they're a conversational tool." A few people questioned this statement, asking how a form of reading could be nonliterate. My point was that I believe most people don't go to the Internet to read. We go to the Web to play games, interact with a friend, and scan for information. The Internet is more about making a connection than reading for comprehension or enjoyment.

When there's a lot of text on a page, we get impatient and move on. If there are no images or media, then we search elsewhere. We've learned the special skills of sifting through the

Web's endless sea of information to find what we need. We look for bullet points, summaries, and short blips. It has little to do with comprehension—it's search-and-seizure learning.

Instant messaging is even more removed from literacy. It has its own language. The Internet and IM aren't evils to be avoided. I believe they're tools that have the potential to be used for good. I use them every day—probably more than I should! But what I believe most interesting is what they communicate about our culture's values.

The word that many educators are using to describe our culture's approach to reading is not *illiteracy* but *aliteracy*. *Aliteracy* is "the quality or state of being able to read but uninterested in doing so."[20] It's an indifference and boredom with reading for academic and enrichment purposes.

Aliteracy is a choice, a value, or a perceived lack of value in reading. *A Washington Post* article estimated that 50 percent of literate Americans chose *not* to read as a means for learning and enjoyment. Some say the estimate should be closer to 70 percent.[21]

It seems Americans are beginning to find reading unimportant. My wife specializes in helping elementary students embrace reading for enjoyment first—and then for learning. She's noticed that as her students get older and advance into the middle school years, they tend to stop reading for enjoyment and see reading as just a means to gain information. This is a constant, uphill battle for our educational system as it tries to paddle against the stream of culture—and the examples of most parents. A lot has changed in just a few decades.

Communications expert Marshall McLuhan, famous for his statement "The medium is the message," foresaw the beginnings of this shift in our culture 40 years ago:

> We now live in the early part of an age for which the meaning of print culture is becoming as alien as the meaning of manuscript culture was to the eighteenth century. We're primitives of a new culture...there is a new electric technology that threatens this ancient technology of literacy built upon the phonetic alphabet. Our Western values, built on the written word, have already been considerably affected by the electric media...Perhaps that's the reason why many highly literate people in our time find it difficult to examine this question without getting into a moral panic.[22]

Richard Jensen describes this as a "communication revolution" in his landmark book *Thinking in Story: Preaching in a Post-Literate Age*:

A TRUE STORY ABOUT STORYING

I grew up going to church and Sunday school where I heard many Bible stories. In fact, not only did I hear those stories, but I actually saw them played out on a flannelgraph with one-dimensional figures of Abraham, Moses, and Jesus. I felt I had a pretty good understanding of the details of the Bible, but I was never really caught up in the adventure.

Years later when I was attending Bible college, I served as a youth leader at my church. This was the first time I heard my youth pastor talk about "God's Story," introducing us to a series of 12 primitively drawn—but memorable—symbols, each depicting a key episode from the Bible. (I found out later that he'd gotten these symbols from Michael Novelli.) At the same time, I clearly began to see a "redemptive arc" from creation to new creation as I was taking Old and New Testament Survey courses. The Bible was becoming less disjointed for me, and I loved discovering all of the connections and synergy within Scripture.

Our youth ministry began to use those episodic symbols as a way to tell and discuss God's Story, helping our students to understand the whole gospel instead of focusing solely on Jesus' birth, death, and resurrection. Our youth group was now getting grounded in the importance of Jesus' life and death in the context of God's activity throughout history. We even used the symbols and their corresponding narratives to share the gospel with a sister church in the Dominican Republic.

A couple of years later, I was sitting in a meeting to help plan the first Merge Toronto event with Michael and Caesar. They began leading our team of staff and volunteers through the storying process, which would be the basis for this new event. As Michael led us through the creation story, I found myself engaged in a new way. As this group of veteran pastors and youth workers dialogued about this story we'd heard so many times before, something suddenly awoke in me. It was bigger than the details and connections we were making from the story. I was drawn in, and the story became my own—I became caught up by this new adventure. That day, as I continued to hear and discuss the narratives, the Bible became more than history, more than a textbook—it was living and active. God's Word and Spirit were speaking to and through us as we dialogued about God's purposes, and God was inviting our participation in this story.

Many of the young people in our group have felt as though reading the Bible is more of a chore than a privilege. After hearing, discussing, and experiencing God's Story, many expressed to me new enthusiasm and interest in reading the Bible. One student named Jackie said, with no small amount of surprise at her own admission, "I'm actually excited to get home and read my Bible!" Jackie has been digging into her one-year Bible, and she's eager to continue learning the whole Story of God.

I'm aware—now more than ever—that we're a part of the "greatest story ever told." The value of reading and teaching the Bible in narrative form is now an ongoing part of my life. When talking to friends and colleagues about Bible study curricula, I suggest storying. Who better to teach the ways of God than God? What better textbook than God's very Word, and what greater communicator than the Holy Spirit?

I love stories in all of their various formats; but the one that moves and excites me the most is the one that transforms me into a princess, a peacemaker, a missionary. The one in which I'm pursued and loved beyond my wildest dreams. The one in which I'm the daughter of a King, the bride of Christ, the friend of God. The one in which I'm rescued and am now charged with being hope to others in bondage. The best story is the one that I don't just read or watch—I'm called to be a part of it. And this story, God's Story, isn't finished—the King, our Savior, our Friend is writing a new chapter every day.

—MELISSA MORRISSEY, VOLUNTEER IN TORONTO, ONTARIO

Nearly all the experts in communication agree that the world has experienced three communication eras. The first era was an era of oral communication; the second began with writing and continued with print; the third is the era of electronic communication which is now coming to birth…The unique reality of our generation is that we are living on the forefront of a shift from one communication era to another. We are living on the boundary between the print era and the electronic era. This is a revolution. It is a revolution that calls upon us to seriously re-think most of what we do. It is certainly a revolution that calls us to reinvestigate preaching in our time… Ideas must give way to images, and understanding must give way to experience. Preaching must adopt a new kind of language—a language of narrative and emotion. We should be guided by a language of image and suggestion rather than one of rationality, deductive organization, and logic.[23]

phonetic alphabet > libraries > philosophy > post offices > printing press > telephones > radios > televisions > computers

Oral Communication **Pre-literates** **Events / Stories**	Print Communication **Literates** **Words / Ideas**	Digital Communication **Post-literates** **Images / Stories**
Learn through observing, imitating, retelling and dialogue - apprenticeships	*Learn through reading, individual studying and analyzing*	*Learn by hearing, seeing and interacting; experiences move them to belief*
Shared experiences determine truth	*Facts determine truth focused on individual application*	*Personal experiences determine truth*
Get information from stories; use stories to package information	*Get information from print and lecture*	*Get information through media and dialogue*
Driven by events and relationships - a search for connection	*Driven by concepts and principles - a search for knowledge*	*Driven by interaction, participation and imagery - a search for significance*
Think in metaphors	*Thinks linear, analytical, logical*	*Thinking is non-linear, - makes random connections*

Chart developed by Michael Novelli using information from *Thinking in Story*, Richard A. Jensen, 43–44 and "Orality and the Post-Literate West," by Dr. Orville Boyd Jenkins, http://orvillejenkins.com/orality/postliterate.html

The first communication revolution began around 500 BC with the formation of the first library by the Greeks. This spurred a new perspective in Western culture to value written communication over oral, championing reason and philosophy.[24] The ability to see words together on a page, analyze them, and formulate them into categories and outlines gave the Greek culture's upper class a sense of control and finality over words.[25] This perspective shaped a new worldview for many cultures to hold left-brained thinking (rational, analytical) above right-brained thinking (artistic, holistic, intuitive, and creative). Literacy became a source of power and identity for many Western cultures—a defining line between nations and socioeconomic classes.

In 1438 AD, the literate age took full shape when Johannes Gutenberg created "movable type" printing to mass-produce Bibles. Printing opened the door to the Reformation, the age of science, popular education, and ultimately the Industrial Revolution, taking us into what McLuhan called "the Gutenberg Galaxy." We're now in the midst of the second major communication revolution in history—a fast-paced transition from the print era to the digital era. This shift began with the inventions of radio and telephone, continuing with the birth of television and computers and the Internet—drastically changing the way we communicate and process information. While some cultures have remained oral cultures (pre-literate) throughout history, many of the countries in the world have been influenced by these shifts.

This digital era is distinguished by a never-ending flurry of technological developments. Words, music, images, and touch are being multiplexed as media merge them together.

This digital era is distinguished by a never-ending flurry of technological developments. Words, music, images, and touch are being multiplexed as media merge them together. Writing and reading are becoming a means to manipulate other media.

It would be easy for us to cast the transition to a digital era solely in a negative light. Our tendency might be to focus on a disinterest in literacy and call our culture lazy, fat, and unmotivated. But we must look at the glass as being half full, seeing the positive sides of a digital era and the potential advantages for connecting with a student culture.

McLuhan said in his book *The Medium Is the Massage: An Inventory of Effects* that one must understand the workings of the media if one is to understand social and cultural change: "Societies have always been shaped more by the nature of the media by which men communicate than by the content of the communication...The alphabet and print technology fostered and encouraged a fragmenting process, a process of specialism and of detachment. Electric technology fosters and encourages unification and involvement."[26]

This new era also places a high emphasis on image and story. Educator Walter Ong calls this era "secondary-orality" because so many values parallel the pre-literate oral communication era—namely, a returned emphasis on narrative.[27]

Stories are the buzz in business and in Hollywood. Everyone is talking about stories. Marketers and news services have figured out that they need to tell stories. Movies and TV are largely story formats. As trendy as it may seem, there is an underlying effectiveness to stories. These visual media have had a part in "liberating" Western literate societies from being overly focused on literary communication to embrace experience, interaction, and relational values. We'll unpack that more in the next few chapters.

ADAPTING COMMUNICATION TO CULTURE

In *Thinking in Story*, Richard Jensen writes, "People are being changed by their media. In order to speak to changed people, the Church must speak in changed ways."[28]

From the Bible we can see that the apostle Paul adapted his approach to sharing truth through reason in order to reach a Greco-Roman culture that was steeped in philosophy and proposition. For hundreds of years, Paul's approach has been studied and adapted in efforts to reach the literate cultures of the West and beyond.

It seems that further adaptation is now needed in order to effectively reach cultures that learn best from stories and images, rather than words and ideas. Communicating with students is becoming ever more complex and requires lots of creativity. Students today are multi-model learners, instinctively engaging in multiple learning channels simultaneously. New approaches are now required in order to engage students with means that will help them connect and learn.

In *The Second Coming of the Church*, George Barna writes:

For years we have been exposing Christians to scattered, random bits of biblical knowledge through our church services and Christian education classes. They hear a principle here and read a truth there, then nod their head in approval and feel momentarily satisfied over receiving this new insight into their faith. But within the space of just a few hours that principle or truth is lost in the busyness and complexity of their lives. They could not capture that insight and own it because they have never been given sufficient context and method that would enable them to analyze, categorize, and utilize the principle or truth.[29]

This shift in communication causes us to consider—

- Is our method of communicating really helping people to take hold of God's truth—or is what we teach lost in just a few days or hours?

- God's truth is transformational—do our methods complicate things rather than give people context and illumination?

- Does the listener easily pass on our current method of communication? Is it reproducible? Is it helping us make disciples who make disciples?

There are no easy answers to these questions. However, it seems apparent that we need to examine our methods in light of the current communication revolution.

If researchers are correct, then many of our teaching methods use a communication approach that's ineffective for reaching more than half of the people in the United States. It appears that the majority of the world and people within our own culture connect best through stories and less so through concepts and proposition.

In *Rising from the Ashes: Rethinking Church*, author Becky Garrison interviewed a number of leaders in both emergent and mainline churches. One of the questions she asked them was, "How do you see technology (blogs, podcasts) as tools to advance the gospel?" Brian McLaren replied:

Because there is so much explosion of new technology, it's a good time for us to go back to the writings of Marshall McLuhan, the philosopher of technology... McLuhan said that every innovation is an amputation. For example, when you invent the wheel, your legs become weaker. When you invent the television, your ability to become present becomes weaker. When you invent the amplifier, your voice becomes weaker. We need to reflect on this powerful insight and ask, In what ways is technology subtracting or amputating just at the moment we think it's adding and empowering? We should always use it with care, remembering that Jesus modeled personal incarnation, not projection and amplification. I don't know exactly what impact the Internet will have on the local church, for example, but it will have an impact in many areas, including education. Internet-based people know that information is ubiquitous, and they feel empowered to seek it out. They don't need you to spoon-feed them information in lectures like they used to; they can Google it way faster. They need you to do other things…to help them sift through the information, integrate it, incarnate it, reflect on it, model it.[30]

QUESTIONS FOR RESPONSE AND DISCUSSION

Take a moment and look back at the chart that appeared earlier in the chapter. Which of these methods of communication and learning are most natural for you?

Which do you believe is the most natural method of communication for the people you minister to? Think of some examples of how they communicate in this way.

What's the primary way your church/ministry teaches truth?

How might you need to rethink your ministry's communication methods?

NOTES

1. The National Assessment of Adult Literacy (NAAL). The 2003 assessment defines *literacy* as "using printed and written information to adequate.ly function at home, in the workplace, and in the community." National Center for Education Statistics, U.S Department of Education's Executive Summary Results from the 2003 National Assessment of Adult Literacy. Pages 4-7 describe the Levels of Literacy, pages 11-13 give overview data from the survey. http://nces.ed.gov/Pubs2007/2007480_1.pdf

2. Grant Lovejoy, Web article, "Can We Accept Official Literacy Statistics at Face Value?" July 20, 2004, http://www.google.com/search?client=safari&rls=en-us&q=Can+We+Accept+Official+Literacy+Statistics+at+Face+Value%3F&ie=UTF-8&oe=UTF-8

3. http://BookStatistics.com (accessed May 15, 2008).

4   Jane M. Healy, Ph.D., "Kids' Brains Must Be Different..." chapter 1 from *Endangered Minds: Why Children Don't Think and What We Can Do About It* (New York: Simon & Schuster, 1990), http://www.enotalone.com/article/5609.html (accessed May 15, 2008).

5. Greg Toppo, "Why Won't Johnny Read?" *USA Today*, 11/18/2003, http://www.usatoday.com/news/education/2003-11-18-why-wont-johnny-read_x.htm (accessed May 15, 2008).

6. National Endowment for the Arts, "To Read or Not To Read: A Question of National Consequence," Research Report #47, November 2007, http://www.nea.gov/research/ToRead.pdf (accessed May 15, 2008).

7. Yankelovich, Inc. and Scholastic Corporation, press release, "New Study Shows That Kids' Reading Drops Off after Age Eight, and That Parents Can Have a Direct Impact on Getting Kids to Read," June 14, 2006, http://www.scholastic.com/aboutscholastic/news/KidsandReadingPressRelase6-141.pdf (accessed May 15, 2008).

8. The Literacy Company, "Reading, Literacy & Education Statistics," http://www.readfaster.com/education_stats.asp (accessed May 15, 2008).

9. The Lausanne Movement, "Fast Facts—Making Disciples of Oral Learners," 2004 Forum Daily Update, October 2, 2004, http://www.lausanne.org/2004-forum/update02102004.html (accessed May 15, 2008).

10. Associated Press, "Average Home Has More TVs than People," USA Today, 9/21/2006, http://www.usatoday.com/life/television/news/2006-09-21-homes-tv_x.htm

11. Committee on Public Education, American Academy of Pediatrics, "Children, Adolescents, and Television," *Pediatrics* 107, no. 2 (2001): 423-426, http://aappolicy.aappublications.org/cgi/content/full/pediatrics;107/2/423 (accessed May 15, 2008).

12. Knowledge Networks/Statistical Research, "How Children Use™ Media Technology 2003," *The Home Technology Monitor*™, https://segueuserfiles.middlebury.edu/fs016a-f03/HCUT_2003_PressSummary.pdf (accessed May 15, 2008).

13. Nielsen Media Research, "35% of U.S. Tweens Own a Mobile Phone, According to Nielsen," http://www.nielsenmedia.com/nc/portal/site/Public/menuitem.55dc65b4a7d5adff3f65936147a062a0/?vgnextoid=885472b6caf96110VgnVCM100000ac0a260aRCRD (accessed May 15, 2008).

14. http://www.frankwbaker.com/media_use.htm (accessed May 15, 2008).

15. WebKnowHow.net, press release, "MySpace and Isobar Debut First Comprehensive Research Study on Social Networks and Marketing," April 23, 2007, http://www.webknowhow.net/news/press/070423SocialNetworkingStudy.html (accessed May 15, 2008).

16. Alexandra Rankin Macgill, Pew Internet / Pew Internet & American Life Project, Data Memo, October 24, 2007, http://www.pewinternet.org/pdfs/PIP_Teen_Parents_data_memo_Oct2007.pdf (accessed May 15, 2008).

17. Amanda Lenhart, Mary Madden, and Paul Hitlin, Pew Internet / Pew Internet & American Life Project, "Teens and Technology: Youth Are Leading the Transition to a Fully Wired and Mobile Nation, July 27, 2005, http://www.pewinternet.org/report_display.asp?r=162 (accessed May 15, 2008).

18. The Harrison Group, whose 2006 Teen Trends study was sponsored by VNU Business Media, surveyed 1,000 Americans aged 13 to 18 on their thoughts and habits, to extrapolate trends for the estimated 25.2 million teens in the United States. This is the third year of the study. From press release, "Flagship Study of America's Youth Describes What Teens Want" / 2006 *Harrison Group/VNU Teen Trend Report* Investigates the World of Generation Y. http://www.harrisongroupinc.com/youth (no longer available online) accessed 10/12/2006; referenced at http://www.news.com/Teens-and-media-a-full-time-job/2100-1041_3-6141920.html

19. John Markoff, Bits (Business Innovation Technology Society) Page, "The Passion of Steve Jobs," The New York Times, January 15, 2008, http://bits.blogs.nytimes.com/2008/01/15/the-passion-of-steve-jobs (accessed May 15, 2008).

20. Merriam-Webster OnLine, http://www.merriam-webster.com/dictionary/aliteracy (accessed May 15, 2008).

21. Linton Weeks, "The No-Book Report: Skim It and Weep: More and More Americans Who Can Read Are Choosing Not To. Can We Afford to Write Them Off?" *Washington Post*, May 14, 2001, http://www.washingtonpost.com/ac2/wp-dyn/A23370-2001May13 (accessed May 15, 2008).

22. Marshall McLuhan, *The Gutenberg Galaxy: The Making of Typographic Man*, (Toronto: UT Press, 1962), 10-11.

23. Richard A. Jensen, *Thinking in Story: Preaching in a Post-literate Age* (Lima, Ohio: CSS Publishing, 1993), 8, 53.

24. Walter J. Ong, *Orality and Literacy: The Technologizing of the Word*, New Accents. ed. (New York: Routledge, 1988), 23.

25. Ibid, 123.

26. Marshall McLuhan and Quentin Fiore, *The Medium Is the Massage: An Inventory of Effects*, New Ed ed. (Corte Madera, Calif: Gingko Press, 2005), 104.

27. Walter J. Ong, *Orality and Literacy: The Technologizing of the Word*, New Accents. ed. (New York: Routledge, 1988), 145.

28. Richard A. Jensen, *Thinking in Story: Preaching in a Post-literate Age* (Lima, Ohio: CSS Publishing, 1993), 43.

29. George Barna, *The Second Coming of the Church: A Blueprint for Survival* (Nashville, Tenn.: Thomas Nelson, 1998), 122.

30. Becky Garrison, "Technology and the Gospel," excerpt from her book *Rising from the Ashes: Rethinking Church*, from *Christianity Today*, January (Web-only) 2008, vol. 52, posted January 9, 2008, http://www.christianitytoday.com/ct/2008/januaryweb-only/102-33.0.html (accessed May 15, 2008).

CONNECTING WITH STORY
CHAPTER 6

> No matter where one travels in this world,
> people love to tell and listen to stories...
> All enjoy entering the life experiences of others through stories...
> Whether used to argue a point, interject humor,
> illustrate a key insight, comfort a despondent friend,
> challenge the champion,or simply pass the time of day,
> a story has a unique way of finding its way into the conversation.
>
> —TOM STEFFEN[1]

Stories are the language of our world...everyone connects with stories. They're the most natural and powerful ways we have to communicate. Good stories capture our imaginations—they draw us in and we begin to feel what the characters feel: Their pain becomes our pain, their victory becomes our victory. We enter stories and make them part of our experience. I've heard that even our brains are organized into stories. That makes sense—when I try to remember something, my thought process is more akin to scanning through visual stories than flipping through files or lists of information.

Take a moment and think about your favorite story from your childhood. It could be a family story that was passed down through the generations or a story from a book. *Who told you this story? What did you like about it? Who was your favorite character?*

Now, think about one of your favorite stories today. It could be from a movie or novel—whatever pops into your mind first. *What is interesting about this story? How does the story make you feel? How do you relate to the story?*

In *Christ Plays in Ten Thousand Places*, author Eugene Peterson writes:

> Story is the most natural way of enlarging and deepening our sense of reality, and then enlisting us as participants in it. Stories open doors to areas or aspects of life that we didn't know were there, or had quit noticing out of over-familiarity, or supposed were out-of-bounds to us. They then welcome us in. Stories are verbal acts of hospitality.[2]

We sometimes underestimate the power of story because stories are implicit in nature. Without us realizing it, a story can get under our skin, influence our thoughts, and stir our emotions. Stories have the power to—

- Provoke interest and curiosity
- Invite participation
- Encourage community and laughter
- Challenge the way we think and live
- Move and shape us
- Help us remember
- Connect us with our common origins
- Link experiences to facts
- Provide context and structure
- Help us understand our common struggle
- Stir our hearts toward empathy and compassion
- Spark our imaginations and inspire us to hope

In his book *Experiential Storytelling*, Mark Miller writes:

> Storytelling is powerful because it has the ability to touch human beings at the most personal level. While facts are viewed from the lens of a microscope, stories are viewed from the lens of the soul. Stories address us on every level. They speak to the mind, the body, the emotions, the spirit, and the will. In a story a person can identify with situations he or she has never been in. The individual's imagination is unlocked to dream what was previously unimaginable.[3]

Throughout history, societies have passed on their values, beliefs, and traditions through stories. Woven into the fabric of our cultures, families, and communities, they're the strands that bind us together. Stories define who we are. Story is at the core of our identities and is the essence of our memories. We live in stories.

Each person is born with the innate ability to learn and share through stories. By the time a child is about three years old, she can tell many kinds of stories, recall stories she's heard, and even make up her own stories. Story is ingrained in us and is a critical part of our development.

When children listen to stories, they respond by imagining the characters and places described by the words in their minds. According to psychologist Jerome Bruner, children "turn things into stories, and when they try to make sense of their life they use the storied version of their experience as the basis for further reflection. If they don't catch something in a narrative structure, it doesn't get remembered very well, and it doesn't seem to be accessible for further kinds of mulling over."[4]

Even well into adulthood, we find it easier to process information in narrative form than in more abstract forms such as equations and graphs. Most effective of all are narratives that we construct ourselves.

During a Library of Congress lecture, Robert Ornstein, a leading psychologist and professor at Stanford, said—

> Stories are designed to embody—in their characters, plots, and imagery—patterns and relationships that nurture a part of the mind that's unreachable in more direct ways, thus increasing our understanding and breadth of vision, in addition to fostering our

ability to think critically. Stories activate the right side of the brain much more than… reading normal prose. The right side of the brain provides "context," the essential function of putting together the different components of experience. The left side provides the "text," or the pieces themselves.[5]

Story unlocks a part of us that's essential to giving shape and context to life. It unleashes our imaginations and creativity—necessary to deep learning and experience. I've often wondered if we can fully embrace a spiritual truth without it being processed by our imaginations. It seems to me that imagination is a key to faith. We must creatively form ideas and images in our minds in order to give meaning to them. I don't mean to say that faith is imaginary. On the contrary, it brings to reality that which is not present to our senses.

Story helps us tap into our imaginations, unleashing the part of us that processes meaning and the abstract, metaphors and analogies, helping us as we try to grasp the invisible and indefinable. Story helps us go beyond learning that's just knowledge to learning that's embodied.

Linda Fredericks, education and volunteer training expert, describes imagination's role in learning this way:

> This process of developing internal images and meaning in response to words is the basis of imagination…The capacity for imagination has profound implications, not just for academic learning, but for behavior as well. Several recent studies have shown that children who lack imagination are far more prone to violence. Such children cannot imagine alternatives to their immediate perceptions of anger or hostility; they're able to react only to what they believe is the situation in front of them. On the other hand, children who possess imagination have a very different experience. They can be exposed to the same hostile situation as an aggressive child, but with their ability to imagine, different solutions can be reached.[6]

Both my wife and I have been involved in the education of adolescents in one form or another for the last 15 years. During that time, particularly in American public education, an unmistakable shift has taken place toward embracing learner-centered methods. Lectures have been replaced with hands-on learning, group projects, and stories. Curricula are being adapted to accommodate multiple learning styles. It seems as though the U.S. educational system has identified the value of interaction and participation in education that defines this digital age.

A big emphasis on narrative and stories is now being used in teaching. Educators have noticed that storytelling sparks creativity and participation, develops listening skills, improves vocabulary and reading, and helps strengthen critical thinking skills.[7]

No other medium addresses varied learning styles like storytelling does. Educators are realizing that stories can be used as a powerful and memorable vehicle to convey facts. Many creative approaches are being used to implement narrative in schools today. My wife's class used stories to help connect math to real-life scenarios, and she found that this approach worked much more effectively than conventional methods for teaching math concepts.

In an article entitled "'Hamlet' Too Hard? Try a Comic Book," Teresa Méndez, staff writer for *The Christian Science Monitor*, writes:

> At Oneida High School in upstate New York, Diane Roy teaches students who failed ninth-grade English the first time around. Last year, on the heels of "Hamlet," she presented her class with a graphic novel—essentially a variety of comic book…Each student was required to read five graphic novels. "There wasn't a single student in this class of kids—nonreaders who don't enjoy reading—who didn't read double that number," Roy says. "They would read them overnight…they were reading them at lunch, in the hallway."[8]

Graphic novels use a combination of media—images and words—to connect students to a story in a new way. Japanese graphic novels, called Manga, have become hugely popular with young readers and are now becoming bestsellers among teenagers in the United States.

The call to use story is a call to engage students' imaginations instead of just presenting information and motivation. It's a call to explore creative means that merge words, images, and sounds to bring life transformation.

LIVING IN GOD'S STORY

One of the most important questions we can ask is, *What story is my life a part of?* There are many competing stories in our world, and people are confronted with the idea of which ones they should give their lives to. Whether there is a conscious choice or not, we choose to give our lives to some story. One of my favorite quotes is by author Stephen Shoemaker from his book *GodStories*: "Our lives must find their place in some greater story or they will find their place in some lesser story. Our contemporary post-modern world is a world of a thousand stories and a thousand gods. And these stories become splintered images, brilliant, excitable, beautiful perhaps, but separated from any larger narrative to give them meaning and truth."[9]

Author Lesslie Newbigin, in his book *The Gospel in a Pluralist Society*, writes, "The way we understand human life depends on what conception we have of the human story. What is the real story of which my life is a part?"[10]

Newbigin continues,

> In our contemporary culture…two quite different stories are told. One is the story of evolution, of the development of species through the survival of the strong, and the story of the rise of civilization, our type of civilization, and its success in giving humankind mastery of nature. The other story is one embodied in the Bible, the story of creation and fall, of God's election of a people to be the bearers of his purpose for humankind, and of the coming of the one in whom that purpose is to be fulfilled. These are two different and incompatible stories.[11]

These competing stories are called *meta-narratives*, overarching accounts that give shape to history and provide meaning to human life. Each has a set of values and goals—calling us to come and live in its story. Each has the power to shape our thoughts, actions, and world-view. But when we try to mix these rivaling stories, it becomes messy—and we find ourselves caught between two worlds with opposing values. We can see examples of this in the Bible, and it's likely that we're familiar with people who've engaged in this struggle throughout history as well. The stories of this world lure us in. They lead us to believe we're self-sufficient. Central to them is a drive for success and status, acquiring material possessions to provide comfort and entertainment. These ideals have defined the American dream for decades, and generations have given themselves to its story. Even as followers of Jesus, the world's

A TRUE STORY ABOUT STORYING

I've been in youth ministry for 11 years, and I'm enjoying it now more than ever. Most of this has to do with my experience with storying. Over the last couple of years, storying has helped me to discover new and meaningful ways to be a spiritual guide for my students and young adults. As we've gone through the stories, I'm encouraged by the depth and meaning that my students share from their lives. Storying provides us with opportunities to share observations and struggles and to reveal what we're grasping from the Bible. By listening to my students share, I've gained tremendous insight into what's going on in their minds and hearts.

Storying has helped me feel free and excited to teach in a new way. It seemed as though teaching in more traditional ways depended so much on what I brought—the right points, the right prop, the right joke, the right video—in order for students to learn. Now, through storying, I feel as though we're partners. I'm continually learning from my group as we move through these sacred stories. Each week a number of the students come back to our group—unprompted—with something they've researched, helping us dig deeper into a part of the story they had questions about or didn't understand.

Storying has helped me really believe that God will speak to and through my students if they'll work to enter the story. This is something I'd lost hope in, but now I continue to see God reveal to us new things about who he is and who we are. God is surprising us with new things we've never thought of before, and God continues to open up our perspectives on how big, mysterious, and beautiful he really is.

As I drove home from the house group last night, I pictured in my mind Anna, Todd, Ricky, Alex, and many of the other students who were there. I was moved by the experience we'd shared together as a diverse group—students and adults who are black, Latino, or white; some are rich, some are middle class, and some are poor; there are people who are attending college, struggling in high school, or dropping out of high school.

For the first time in more than a decade of ministry, I've found a way to connect people with the complex, deep truths found in the Bible. God has reminded me again that wherever two or more of us are together, God is present, lovingly speaking and revealing himself to us.

—SETH MCCOY, YOUTH WORKER IN ST. PAUL, MINNESOTA

competing stories (and kingdoms) can draw us in ever so subtly, influencing our thoughts and actions every day.

The call to view the Bible as one story is, in part, a call to once again see the distinction between these two competing stories. That said, I believe our efforts to systematize the Bible has deterred us from seeing its overarching story—and stripped it of its narrative power.

In other words, we've taken bits and pieces of the Bible and tried to fit them into the predominant humanistic story of our culture (our preaching and Bible study methods attest to this). But we've done it to such an extent that many well-intended churches promote our culture's humanistic story instead of God's. We've become a church that embraces individualism, consumerism, and prosperity—all propped up with Bible passages.

> The Bible is not a mere jumble of history, poetry, lessons in morality and theology, comforting promises, guiding principles and commands; instead, it is fundamentally coherent. Every part of the Bible—each event, book, character, command, prophecy, and poem—must be understood in the context of one story line.
>
> Many of us have read the Bible as if it were merely a mosaic of little bits—theological bits, moral bits, historical-critical bits, sermon bits, devotional bits. But when we read the Bible in such a fragmented way, we ignore its divine author's intention to shape our lives through its story.
>
> All human communities live out some story that provides a context for understanding the meaning of history and gives shape and direction to their lives. If we allow the Bible to become fragmented, it is in danger of being absorbed into whatever other story is shaping our culture, and it will thus cease to shape our lives as it should."[12]

When the Bible is no longer embodied and shared as a true story to give my life to, it's subject to being overcome by the story of the culture. When fragmented and propositionalized, the Bible story risks becoming dull and impotent compared to the powerful message of our culture. We therefore must *retell* God's Story—the better story—and help each other see that God desires a better way for us to live.

Eugene H. Peterson, translator of *The Message*, describes it this way:

Stories are the most prominent biblical way of helping us see ourselves in "the God story," which always gets around to the story of God making and saving us. Stories, in contrast to abstract statements of truth, tease us into becoming participants in what is being said. We find ourselves involved in the action. We may start as spectators or critics, but if the story is good (and the biblical stories are very good!), we find ourselves no longer just listening to but inhabiting the story."[13]

We're called to live in a story that's still unfurling. God is not finished with us yet, thankfully. The Bible story is not just a story from the past; it's a living story, one of vibrancy and dimension. It's incarnational, entering our lives differently than other stories can. God calls us to inhabit the story, allowing it to shape and guide our lives.

Richard Jensen puts it this way:

The stories of the Bible invite us to participate in their reality…not to understand that reality. Participating in the reality of the gospel in story form is something quite different than understanding the gospel in idea form. The fact that we participate in the life of stories means that stories function to bring God's presence into our lives. The gospel in story is a happening-reality. The story works by involving people in its reality. We must simply let the story do its work![14]

OUR ROLE IN GOD'S STORY

As we enter into God's Story as narrative, a whole new world is opened to us. One of the most significant things that happen when we enter into God's Story is that we begin to get a sense of God's entire interconnected narrative, and we see how it intersects with our own stories. The narrative, in turn, clarifies our place in God's Story and helps us take the focus off ourselves and aim it toward God and his desires for the world.

This is in direct contrast to what much of Protestant Christianity in America has focused on for the last several decades. Churches have highlighted an individual and personal faith, pointing toward personal devotions, personal evangelism, and personal growth as benchmarks. This way of thinking contributes to the idea that "God is a part of *my story*." Thus, the goal becomes motivating people to make room for God in their own stories and let God play a bigger part. In other words, make God more central.

This seems like a noble focus in some ways—and it's one that I had for a long time. But now I can see that it's backward. Not only does this way of thinking place my own story as the centerpiece of my life, but it also leads me to a never-ending struggle to put God first. Spiritual formation becomes an individual process, focused on spiritual disciplines, solitude, and surrender. And while disciplines, solitude, and surrender have their place and importance, viewing them so centrally creates a limited perspective.

We need to stop trying to *fit* God into our lives and stories and realize that God desires us to play a role in his Story instead. As subtle a difference as it may seem, the shift in perspective changes *everything*. When we see ourselves as a part of God's Story—as opposed to God being a part of our stories—it awakens us to live in a broader reality, to live for and contribute to something bigger than ourselves.

Furthermore, fitting God into our own stories seems akin to trying to create our own realities—revolving around our own desires—as we ask God to bless our actions. We then invest time and resources trying to find out how the Bible is relevant to *our lives* instead of trying to discover and pursue how we might become more relevant to God's Story already in progress.

God doesn't have a relevance issue—we do!

Again, Eugene Peterson describes this so well:

> The Christian life is not about us; it is about God. Christian spirituality is not a life-project for becoming a better person, it is not about developing a so-called "deeper life." We are in on it, to be sure. But we are not the subject. Nor are we the action… The great weakness of North American spirituality is that it is all about us: fulfilling our potential, getting in on the blessings of God, expanding our influence, finding our gifts, getting a handle on principles by which we can get an edge over the competition. And the more there is of us, the less there is of God.[15]

We're called to join God and his actions in us and in the world, participating in what God is doing. When we get a picture of how our lives fit into the encompassing epic of God's Story, we begin to see our part in God's activity as his people in the world. Our focus changes. We move away from our own agendas to join God in restoring things to wholeness—the way God created them to be. It's a focus that moves beyond personal growth to participation in God's kingdom.

THE BIBLE'S STORYLINE

When I began to get a sense of the entire narrative and see the Bible as one story, a common thread came into focus for me—a storyline that runs through the entirety of Scripture. While many themes and symbols can be found repeated throughout Scripture, none seems more predominant than the kingdom of God. *Kingdom*, in fact, was Jesus' chosen word to describe the community of people who would experience God's reign by living according to God's ways.

My pastor, Joel Kline of Highland Avenue Church of the Brethren in Elgin, Illinois, recently described God's Story as "the alternative story of life in the kingdom of God—an invitation to live, here and now, as if God's kingdom were fully present among us. It is a call to embrace Christ's new story for our living, a story that speaks of new possibilities in God's kingdom—a realm of living based not on oppressive control and domination over others but on bottom-up service; a realm of living marked not by a clenched fist but by open, wounded hands extended in a welcoming embrace of kindness, gentleness, forgiveness, and grace...a realm of living ever seeking to expand the circles of God's renewing love."

From the very beginnings of the story, God expresses a desire to live in close harmony with God's creation and for God's creation to enjoy his kingdom rule. God created humans as image-bearers of the divine, continuing God's creativity and care of creation on earth. Then humans decided to create their own kingdoms, where they could live according to their own desires.

So God set in motion a kingdom agenda to restore creation to wholeness. Story after Bible story describes the amazing lengths God went to in order to extend grace to us—to give humans opportunities to reconnect our broken relationship with him. God even came and dwelled with the Jewish nation—a community God chose to distinctly live while reflecting the ways of God the King.

The apex of the kingdom storyline is found in Jesus. Jesus announced the kingdom of God breaking into history, displaying God's restorative power in his life, miracles, and words. At the cross Jesus gained decisive victory over evil for us, liberating us from the power of sin. Then Jesus entered as the firstborn into the resurrection life of restored creation. God's Spirit was sent to continue the restorative work, empowering a global community of people called the church to embody God's kingdom, join in God's actions, and tell God's Story to the world.

(I provided a summary narrative and some additional resources about the Bible's storyline in Appendix D. This section will help you get a better grasp on the Bible's overarching narrative, and how you can teach it to your group.)

THE ORAL TRADITION

The religious beliefs and cultural traditions of every people group are contained within and passed on through stories. For thousands of years, Jewish and Christian people learned about and experienced God through listening to stories. It's widely accepted that most of the Old Testament Scriptures first existed as oral stories for a long, long time until they were committed to written form in order to be preserved. The books of Moses, for instance, were written no sooner than 700 years after God called Abram to leave Ur and go to the place God would show him. Presumably Abraham's descendants preserved those stories and their chronology by oral means until they were finally written down in books. Christians eventually gathered the inspired writings into compilations called "Bibles," and the Christian church received them as Scripture.[16]

The Hebrew culture didn't use a phonetic alphabet and still remains an oral storytelling culture.[17] Jewish people knew the Scriptures very well from telling and retelling them. The stories they told and listened to were, in fact, their Bible as much—or, some would say, more than—the printed text we have today.[18]

Listeners of the Torah were required to retell it the way they'd been taught. The early church also followed this practice, with families passing down stories of faith to each generation.[19]

Jesus was known as a powerful storyteller, as described in Mark 4:33-34: "With many stories like these, [Jesus] presented his message to them, fitting the stories to their experience and maturity. He was never without a story when he spoke. When he was alone with his disciples, he went over everything, sorting out the tangles, untying the knots" (*The Message*).

In fact, the Bible tells us that "Jesus spoke all these things to the crowd in parables; he did not say anything to them without using a parable" (Matthew 13:34). Parables are stories that draw a parallel to our lives. Jesus used parables to describe life around him, using everyday objects to teach deep truths. He related to a society of farmers and fishermen with stories that were interesting, easy to remember, and life changing. Jesus saw the value of helping others see the big picture of God's Story from the beginning. He related his story to his culture within the context of the grand Story.

One of my favorite references to storytelling in the New Testament is when Jesus was walking on the road to Emmaus shortly after his resurrection (quoted here from Luke 24:27,32, NIV): "And beginning with Moses and all the Prophets, [Jesus] explained to them what was said in all the Scriptures concerning himself...They asked each other, 'Were not our hearts burning within us while he talked with us on the road and opened the Scriptures to us?'"

Jesus was telling them THE story, starting way back with Moses, and connecting the story all the way to their present lives. Jesus knew the power of God's Story and used it to help his disciples find themselves in that Story.

The Bible isn't just full of stories; it's also full of storytellers: Moses (Exodus), David (Psalms 78, 105, 106), Nehemiah (Nehemiah 9), Stephen (Acts 7), and Paul (Acts 13, Galatians 3 and 4), just to name a few. These believers inspired and challenged people with true accounts of God's activity and faithfulness.

It seems that when a culture comes to the Scriptures in an oral rather than written form, it causes them to treat the Scriptures in a different way. The Hebrew culture looked at the Scriptures as stories to live by, carrying the Scriptures in their minds and hearts, listening intently to experience the stories, allowing them to teach, shape, and unify their society.

> **The Hebrew culture looked at the Scriptures as stories to live by, carrying the Scriptures in their minds and hearts, listening intently to experience the stories, allowing them to teach, shape, and unify their society.**

We've lost the beauty and richness of the oral tradition that's a part of our spiritual heritage. I believe that if we strive to regain a focus on experiencing the Scriptures as God's Story, it will help us rediscover our identities as God's people.

RECLAIMING OUR ROLES AS STORYTELLERS

In light of our history and current culture, we have a responsibility to reevaluate our methods of communicating the Bible. I believe that in order to be effective, we must reclaim our roles as storytellers, embracing them in the form of artful narrators and prophetic historians.

ARTFUL NARRATORS

Storytelling is more like the work of an artist than a teacher. It's less about explaining what something means and more about allowing others to explore for themselves. The hope is that listeners will make their own connections between the Story and their own stories, as this has a much greater impact than any connections we might try to make for them. This is different from preaching or teaching in that we're not in total control of the conclusions that others may draw from what we say.

Here are some excerpts that speak to the idea of artful narration.

> As the biblical story unfolds, it does so in stories and poetry. In fact, approximately seventy-five percent of scripture consists of narrative, fifteen percent is expressed in poetic forms and only ten percent is propositional and overtly instructional in nature. In our retelling of the same story, we have reversed this biblical pattern. Today an estimated ten percent of our communication is designed to capture the imagination of the listener, while ninety percent is purely instructive.[20]

> Our literate tradition trained us to find the ideas in the Bible and shape them in logical ways for the preaching task…we have learned how to use Scripture as the source of ideas we wish to inculcate in the life of our people. There is another possibility. We can also fill their heads with people! We can tell biblical stories in such a way that the characters of the Bible come to live in the hearts and minds of our listeners…One of the ways in which Christ can be formed within us is the way of biblical characters living within our consciousness.[21]

> The new conversations, on which our very lives depend, require a poet not a moralist. Because finally church people are like other people; we are not changed by new rules. The deep places in our lives—places of resistance and embrace—are not ultimately reached by instruction. Those places of resistance and embrace are reached only by stories, by images, metaphors and phrases that line out the world differently, apart from fear or hurt.[22]

PROPHETIC HISTORIANS

Is there a place for the teacher and the expert in church today? Yes, I believe there is.

I believe those with the gift of teaching need to major in the art of facilitating discussion (more on that in coming chapters), become artful narrators, and reframe their roles as prophetic historians.

Prophetic what...? Teachers should invest themselves deeply in the study of the ancient cultures of the Bible, so they can bring that world to life in their communities of faith. Prophetic historians give us real insights into the text and help us to enter the world of stories we find there.

Pastor David Fitch describes the new role of preaching this way: "Instead of dissecting the text, making it portable, and distributing it to people for their own personal use, the preacher re-narrates the world as it is under the Lordship of Christ and then invites people into it."[23]

Over the last decade, I believe some new prophetic historians have emerged, including Dan Allender, Rob Bell, Scot McKnight, and Brian McLaren. Whether or not you agree with their theologies, they have unique gifts to help us experience the past and connect their messages to a bigger Story. Prophetic historians are always mindful to place their present content in the context of the broader Story of God.

QUESTIONS FOR RESPONSE AND DISCUSSION

Which parts of this chapter did you relate to your own story?

What was your favorite story during your childhood? Who told you this story? What did you like about it? Who was your favorite character?

Why do you think we connect with stories in such deep ways?

What "stories" do you see the people around you giving their lives to?

How might stories reshape the way you teach and learn from the Bible?

NOTES

1. Tom Steffen, "Storytelling: Why Do It? Is It an Essential Skill for Missionaries?" an excerpt from chapter 8 of *Reconnecting God's Story to Ministry: Cross-Cultural Storytelling at Home and Abroad* (Colorado Springs, Colo.: Authentic, 2005), http://www.missionfrontiers.org (accessed May 15, 2008).

2. Eugene Peterson, *Christ Plays in Ten Thousand Places: A Conversation in Spiritual Theology* (Grand Rapids, Mich.: Eerdmans, 2005), 13.

3. Mark Miller, *Experiential Storytelling: (Re) Discovering Narrative to Communicate God's Message* (Grand Rapids, Mich.: Zondervan/Youth Specialties, 2003), 24.

4. Robert H. Frank, "Students Discover Economics in Its Natural State," New York Times, September 29, 2005, http://www.nytimes.com/2005/09/29/business/29scene.html?ei=5090&en=331feb91619eb770&ex=1285646400&partner=rssuserland&emc=rss&pagewanted=print

5. Robert Ornstein, "Teaching-Stories and the Brain," Library of Congress lecture, 2002.

6. Linda Fredericks, "Developing Literacy Skills Through Storytelling," Corporation for National and Community Service, Spring 1997, http://nationalserviceresources.org/resources/newsletters/resource_connection/volume_2_number_4/developing_literacy.php (accessed May 15, 2008).

7. Ibid.

8. Teresa Méndez, "'Hamlet' Too Hard? Try a Comic Book," Learning Page, Christian Science Monitor Web site, http://www.csmonitor.com/2004/1012/p11s01-legn.html (accessed May 15, 2008).

9. H. Stephen Shoemaker, *Godstories: New Narratives from Sacred Texts* (Valley Forge, Penn.: Judson Press, 1998), xix.

10. Lesslie Newbigin, *The Gospel in a Pluralist Society* (Grand Rapids, Mich: Eerdmans, 1989), 15.

11. Ibid., 15-16.

12. Craig G. Bartholomew and Michael W. Goheen, *The Drama of Scripture* (Baker Academic, Grand Rapids, Mich. 2004), 12.

13. Eugene H. Peterson, Introduction to the Book of Jonah, *The Message Remix*, 2nd Edition (NavPress, Colorado Springs, 2006), 1352.

14. Richard A. Jensen, *Thinking in Story: Preaching in a Post-Literate Age* (CSS Publishing, Lima, Ohio, 1993), 62.

15. Eugene H. Peterson, *Christ Plays in Ten Thousand Places: A Conversation in Spiritual Theology* (Grand Rapids, Mich.: Eerdmans, 2005), 335.

16. Dr. Grant Lovejoy, *Chronological Bible Storying: Description, Rationale and Implications,* A paper presented at the Non-Print Media Consultation in Nairobi, Kenya, June 2000, http://www.churchplantingvillage.net/atf/cf/%7B087EF6B4-D6E5-4BBF-BED1-7983D360F394%7D/Chronological_Bible_Storying_-_A_Description.pdf (accessed May 15, 2008).

17. Richard A. Jensen, *Thinking in Story: Preaching in a Post-Literate Age* (Lima, Ohio: CSS Publishing, 1993), 30.

18. Everett Fox, *The Five Books of Moses: Genesis, Exodus, Leviticus, Numbers, and Deuteronomy* (New York: Schocken Books, 1995), 9.

19. Thomas E. Boomershine, *Story Journey: An Invitation to the Gospel as Storytelling* (Nashville, Tenn.: Abingdon Press, 1988), 141.

20. Colin Harbinson, "Restoring the Arts to the Church: The Role of Creativity in the Expression of Truth," *Lausanne World Pulse Magazine* (online), July 2006, edited from a chapter in *The Complete Evangelism Guidebook,* Scott Dawson ed. (Grand Rapids, Mich: Baker Books, 2006), http://www.lausanneworldpulse.com/themedarticles.php/409/07-2006 (accessed May 15, 2008).

21. Richard A. Jensen, *Thinking in Story: Preaching in a Post-literate Age* (Lima, Ohio: CSS Publishing, 1993), 9.

22. Walter Brueggemann, *Finally Comes the Poet: Daring Speech for Proclamation* (Minneapolis: Augsburg Fortress, 1989), 109-110.

23. David Fitch, "The Myth of Expository Preaching (Part 2): Proclamation That Inspires the Imagination," Out of Ur (conversations hosted by the editors of *Leadership Journal*), *Christianity Today* blog, posted July 25, 2006, http://blog.christianitytoday.com/outofur/archives/2006/07/the_myth_of_exp_1.html (accessed May 15, 2008).

TURNING THE DIAMOND
CHAPTER 7

WHAT IS STORYING?

Storying, short for Chronological Bible Storying, is a sequential telling of Bible stories followed by a time of review and dialogue. This method is based on an ancient Hebrew way of learning through careful observation and discussion.[1]

Storying was introduced a few decades ago by missionaries who felt that understanding and remembering the gospel should not hinge on literacy. (To learn more about the history of Chronological Bible Storying, see Appendix E.)

Recently, storying is also proving to be effective with youth and adults in our media-literate, story-oriented North American context. My hope is to continue to inspire and equip people all over the world to encounter God through his Story.

THE PURPOSE OF STORYING

The purpose of storying is to create an environment for us to connect with God through the whole Bible story. How do we create that environment? I'm glad you asked. We'll unpack that more in later chapters; but, essentially, we create the right environment through a storytelling experience, creative retelling opportunities, and guided discussion that promotes wondering, observations, and connections.

DESIRED OUTCOMES OF STORYING

As we participate in storying, we desire to—

- Become a story-formed community, developing deep friendships with each other

- Listen for and expect God to speak through his Story to and through each other

- See the Bible as one big interconnected story, revealing God's plan to rescue and restore us

- Gain a sense of awe, wonder, and amazement of God

- Discover our identity and role in God's Story—as a distinct people called to live in God's ways

- Fulfill our role as a community, bringing God's blessing and restoration to the world

- Grow in our desire to read and dig deeper into the Bible

- Develop a mental timeline of God's Story, giving context and a foundation for future Bible learning

- Incorporate creative learning methods and expression into our community to connect with varying styles

- Have fun while learning—laugh and enjoy being together

- Encourage more Bible "storyers" to emerge

COMMON QUESTIONS ABOUT STORYING

WHICH STORIES SHOULD I TELL?

While we may not be able to tell *all* of the stories in the Bible, we should give careful consideration to covering a full chronology of stories that will give participants a sense of the entire Bible story. There is no set formula for this, but do your best to provide a set of stories that will help frame up a mental timeline or road map of Scripture.

A WORLDWIDE PHENOMENON

Storying is now used extensively around the world. OneStory (www.onestory.org) is a partnership using storying to reach the most remote and unengaged people groups in the world with Scripture. This partnership includes Campus Crusade for Christ, the International Mission Board of the Southern Baptist Convention, Trans World Radio, Wycliffe International, and YWAM, plus many more organizations, churches, and individuals. OneStory has already begun mobilizing people to do storying in Africa, Asia, Europe, and Latin America.

There are many great resources you can use as you begin storying, and I've provided a list of some of them in the appendices. However, I encourage anyone who's willing and able to stitch together his or her own story sets from the Scriptures.

For those who simply don't have the time to develop their own narratives, you can use resources such as Zondervan's *The Story: Read the Bible as One Seamless Story from Beginning to End.* Or download the 21 narratives I've put together for individual and local church use—free. These stories are my attempts to paint a picture of God's redemptive plan and to help listeners connect with God's Story. You can access them at www.EchotheStory.com.

A TRUE STORY ABOUT STORYING

My deep love for story and for God's timeless truths drew me to the storying process. I'd done all kinds of research on communicating in stories, in wondering, and in questions, but I had yet to experience it. I knew storying would be a great thing, but I didn't realize how deep it would go. Storying connected with my soul— deep into that place where most other things don't have the power to touch.

My first experience with storying was during a training session with Michael in which we were learning how to lead this process. I felt as though this was the first time I'd been able to experience God's Story—able to wonder, to think, to process in a new way. I fell totally in love with God as the Creator and the greatest Artist. I saw more and understood more about God. I experienced the emotion that God expressed in the stories— anger, lament, joy, despair, amazement, hope. The story became a whole experience—not divided in pieces and packaged. It was complete.

We recently began storying with the students at our church, and they've been blown away! Most of the students I work with have never really been to church. But right before my eyes, I've seen seeds being planted and real growth taking place. We've had discussions about the Bible that are incredibly deep—deeper than I had in Bible college. They were taken on a journey into the Story of God, and they were captivated by its complexity and beauty.

I feel as though storying helps free the power of the Bible to speak. I've seen hardened, rebellious kids' eyes light up as they frantically search for paper and pen so they can start writing down what the group is discussing. I'm watching teenagers fall in love with Jesus. They're connecting like I've never seen before. They're realizing they have a place in this amazing story. God's Story is helping our students grow in a deep understanding of God and an unshakable relationship with him.

—HEATHER FROMAN, VOLUNTEER IN CHICAGO, ILLINOIS

In developing these narratives, my goal was to remain true to the biblical texts, preserving key events and dialogue. I hope these stories will be a bridge to get people excited about reading and digging into the stories of the Bible. I did my best not to embellish them with my own exposition, addition, elaboration, or cultural perspectives. I wasn't trying to "modernize" the stories but tell them chronologically and accurately.

I spent months comparing English translations as I stitched together each narrative, largely basing the content on the New International Version and New Living Translation. In certain spots, key truths may be emphasized or repeated to draw out a character's qualities.

One of the things that should define us as followers of Jesus is a posture of humility...especially in our approach to the Scriptures. I'll be the first to tell you that I don't have the Bible all figured out. My narratives probably don't contain every detail that every reader would want in them. Bottom line: I hope I never stop listening and learning from the Scriptures, seeing new insights, and discovering new things from new friends. My narratives are certainly a work in progress. I would love to learn from you! (You can contact me at michael@ EchoTheStory.com).

WHY NOT TELL STORIES STRAIGHT FROM THE BIBLE?

Whenever possible, I tell Bible stories directly from the text. Many of the narratives in my Echo story set mirror the modern translations. But most of the Bible—even the narrative parts—is difficult to read aloud, especially conversationally.

Here are some of the challenges that prompted me to weave together these condensed narratives:

Length—The sheer length of the Bible can be intimidating. Where else do we hand people a book the size of a dictionary and ask them to get excited about studying it? Many Bible stories are dozens of chapters long, making them difficult to unpack in a group setting.

Translation—Painstaking efforts have been made to translate and retranslate the Bible, keeping it as close to the original text as possible. I believe God has protected this process. However, anytime a document is translated, there are challenges in making it readable and conversational without sacrificing accuracy. Our English translations aren't very conversational or easy to read—that's why so many paraphrased translations have surfaced.

Language—Even with modern translations, many words and phrases remain unfamiliar to us. Much of what's written in the Bible is tied so closely to past cultures and languages that it's easy for us to get lost and confused. Think about this: It's difficult for us to read and comprehend Shakespeare, which was written in English only a few hundred years ago. The language gap we face with the Bible is even greater.

Tense—Within one story, authors sometimes shift from past to present to future tense. In some cases this is because the accounts were written much later, and the author decided to embed some truths into the text to emphasize different attributes. However, these tense shifts make it difficult to follow some narrative parts of the Bible without getting lost.

Writing Styles—Even if we concentrated on just the Bible's narrative parts, we'd still find that those sections were written in different styles. Some are straightforward historical accounts, some are poetic, and some are written like a novel. The challenge is that some of these styles are mixed together in the same narrative, making them difficult to engage with.

Culture Authorship—Different authors committed the Scripture to written form at different times. So not only is our culture vastly different, but many of the Bible's authors also lived in different cultures and eras. What makes reading the Bible even more challenging is the fact that the authors assumed that those who'd hear or read their words would have an understanding of the cultural distinctives of that time. Without understanding the background of the author and his intended audience, we can become confused and sidetracked.

IS STORYING BIBLICALLY ACCURATE?

I've met with some ministry leaders who are concerned that storying encourages people to abandon Bible reading. They fear that learning Scripture from condensed Bible stories makes people vulnerable to inaccuracies. I've been told, "People need to learn from the actual Bible, not from paraphrased stories."

I understand this concern—it's true that oral Bible stories can be altered more easily than written or printed stories. I had similar concerns when I began the storying process, especially after seeing my students distort the Bible during our inductive studies. And that's why I put painstaking efforts into the narratives I use. I encourage you to do the same.

I'm relieved to say that my experience has been the opposite of what I initially expected; by developing a culture of careful listening in our group, students are very attentive to the details of the story and protective of its accuracies.

What I've learned is that storying promotes "communal correcting." This is when a group helps each other to ensure that important details of the stories are recounted accurately and not overlooked. During the retelling of one of these stories, I've observed individuals miss key parts or say something that's just flat-out wrong. But each time this happened, the group would respond and correct the person before I could, redirecting the conversation right back to the story. And most of the time, all I needed to say was something like, "What do you think about that?" or "Did the story tell us something about this?"

What's more, communal correcting is easier for the group members to handle and accept. When a leader corrects, group members often want to withdraw from the discussion altogether. But communal correction just becomes a refining part of the conversation. I wonder if this process of refinement also played a significant role in the preservation of the Scriptures as they were passed down orally from generation to generation.

You may be thinking, *How could oral stories remain accurate after being retold again and again?* This idea seems foreign to us because we've lived in a culture that's reliant upon printed words. It's easy for us to forget that most people didn't have access to Bibles until several hundred years ago. That noted, I believe our culture's love affair with words over the past century has influenced many to be hyperprotective of the Bible, appointing themselves gatekeepers to preserve its accuracies and use. And while I understand that we're to seek God for discernment and be watchful of false teachings, I also believe it's *God's job* to protect the Story that God inspired. Thus, we need to seek God for wisdom, illumination, and guidance to help us see what God desires us to see in the Bible.

THE BIBLE IS ABOUT REAL EVENTS

The Bible is an interpretation of history. It isn't a history book but an eyewitness account, inspired by God, to reveal part of God's nature and the nature of humans. The Bible is a living document, and it contains real stories—testimonies, journeys, witnesses of God's work and God's people. It provides the story of a religious faith that's not limited by facts and figures.

The Bible isn't a textbook, nor does it claim to be. It largely comes from an age that was pre-science and pre-history. It's the recorded experience and understanding of God by an ancient people over the course of many centuries. The Bible was written over a period of 1,200 years with authors who were kings, farmers, poets, warriors, prophets, slaves, and politicians, to name a few—a huge range of expressions. It tells a single story—the story of a Creator and this Creator's unstoppable love for his creation.

When we enter storying, it's important that we approach it with the mindset that these are real events that actually happened. In order to really stand under the narratives, we must see them as events that happened in the same world in which we now live. Otherwise, the story becomes just a moral lesson or allegory. While moral lessons are helpful, the Bible calls us to much more. It's a call to connect with it—past, present, and future—as *our story*.

THE BIBLE IS A MASHUP OF STORIES—OR A "WIKISTORY"

It'd be nice if the Bible read like a novel from cover to cover. But it's not a novel. It's a series of books that have been grouped together—and many of them are out of chronological order.

In technological terminology, a *mashup* is a Web application that combines data from more than one source into a single integrated tool. The Bible is like this—a mashup of different writings from different authors inspired to tell the unified Story of God and his love for people.

In a recent talk, author Scot McKnight suggested we look at the Bible as a "Wikistory," in which there is "ongoing reworking of the biblical story by new authors who each tell the story in their own way." McKnight continued, "None [of the books of the Bible] is exhaustive, comprehensive or absolute...they are different stories of THE Story. We don't have to harmonize them or try to reconcile them. They're just doing their own versions of the Story, and each has a place in the larger picture."[2]

Let's face it—the Bible is often difficult to read and to teach. We've got our work cut out for us if we wish to give our students a sense of its overarching story. That's why storying is the best way I've found to give people, young and old alike, a Bible overview with context to all future Bible learning.

STORYING RENEWS INTEREST IN BIBLE READING

In America we're fast moving away from being a culture centered on literacy and print communications. It's a huge challenge to strive toward being a people who are shaped by the Bible when we live in a culture that's becoming impatient with reading. Therefore, I believe the solution is not to abandon Scripture reading, but rather reintroduce the Bible to our communities of faith through creative means.

That's precisely the role that Bible storying plays in a postliterate culture. Storying is a bridge that helps people see the Bible in a new way—a gateway that fosters imagination and sparks curiosity to explore the rest of the story. I've seen storying effectively renew interest in Bible reading. So many of my students will go back after our storying times and read the Bible accounts on their own, unprompted. They didn't do this to uncover a nugget of truth or the main plot; they read them as *true stories*—slowing down so they could digest the words and allow the stories to form in their imaginations.

TURNING THE DIAMOND

The Hebrew tradition possesses a unique reverence for God's Story. This manifested itself in the special ways in which they learned from the Scriptures. The Jewish people were taught to regard the Scriptures as a "living person"—with respect and complexity—and take the time to get to know her. They were to approach the stories of the Torah as if they were actually standing in the place of their ancestors—in the presence of God.[3]

Stephen M. Wylen's book *The Seventy Faces of Torah* describes a way in which the Jews studied the text:

> *Shiv'im panim laTorah*—"There are seventy faces to the Torah." Every single verse in the Torah yields seventy different interpretations. Each interpretation teaches something new and different. They may even contradict one another...Yet each one of the seventy interpretations is the true word of God.
>
> The image of the seventy faces may be taken from the imagery of the jeweler's art. Each side of a cut gem is called a facet, a little face. A light sparkles within every fine gemstone. We know that this light is a reflection, but the ancients thought of the light in a gemstone as originating from within the stone. The beauty and fascination of a fine gem is that one stone sparkles in so many different ways. We know there is a single light within the stone, but we see that light differently depending on which face we gaze upon. One diamond is like seventy different diamonds as we turn it, but of course it is one. In the same way there is only one God, whose light shines

forth from every verse in the Torah. We see that light differently depending on how we interpret the verse. The unitary light of God's Holy Spirit is fully revealed in many sparkles and flashes, as we seek God through a multitude of interpretations on every single verse of Scripture.[4]

The Hebrew nation believed that every time they looked at the stories of the Scriptures, they'd discover something new: Further beauty, details, depth, and richness. As they gathered to listen and look attentively into the Scriptures, they'd engage in lively dialogue, sharing all that they'd seen reflected back to them in the 70 faces of Torah. These were spirited discussions, sometimes turning toward disagreement, with shouting and laughter being common-place.[5] Many Jews continue this tradition with the belief that God continues to reveal more of himself each time they gather and learn from the Scriptures.

We, too, should embrace this approach to the Scriptures. The Bible and its stories are living, filled with endless meaning and mystery that we can connect with today. We must listen as God's Spirit illuminates the Scriptures for us—turning the diamond—allowing our imaginations to explore them and the implications of the story to settle on us.

Our community of faith is integral to this process. Author Stephen Fowl writes that "faithful interpretation requires vigilant communities that engage in regular practices of truth telling, forgiveness, and reconciliation with people who posses both humility and the ability to listen well."[6]

Storying helps create this kind of environment, one in which the Spirit can speak through the imaginations of the community, encouraging a broad range of voices to share what God is illuminating to them through his Story.

QUESTIONS FOR RESPONSE AND DISCUSSION

Which parts of this chapter did you relate to your own story?

How do you believe storying might be effective in reaching your culture?

What outcome do you hope for if you use storying with your group?

What might we learn from the ancient Hebrews' approach to Scripture?

NOTES

1. Dr. Grant Lovejoy, *Chronological Bible Storying: Description, Rationale and Implications,* a paper presented at the Non-Print Media Consultation in Nairobi, Kenya, June 2000, http://www.churchplantingvillage.net/atf/cf/%7B087EF6B4-D6E5-4BBF-BED1-7983D360F394%7D/Chronological_Bible_Storying_-_A_Description.pdf (accessed May 15, 2008).

2. From Scot McKnight's message, "Stories on the Story," at the Ancient Evangelical Future Conference, October 2007, http://www.aefcenter.org/attend.html; http://desertpastor.typepad.com/paradoxology/files/McNight_Wiki_Story_short.mp3

3 Stephen M. Wylen, *The Seventy Faces of Torah: The Jewish Way of Reading the Sacred Scriptures* (Mahwah, NJ: Paulist Press, 2005), 62.

4. Ibid., 63.

5. Ibid., 70.

6. David Fitch, "The Myth of Expository Preaching (Part 3): Responding to Scripture as a Community," Out of Ur (conversations hosted by the editors of *Leadership Journal*), *Christianity Today* blog, posted July 28, 2006, http://blog.christianitytoday.com/outofur/archives/2006/07/the_myth_of_exp_2.html (accessed May 15, 2008).

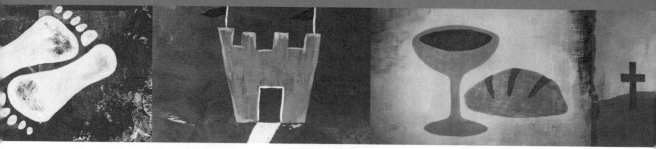

STORYING AND LEARNING
CHAPTER 8

As I visited my wife's school and second-grade classroom, I noticed a significant focus on multiple learning modes. Classrooms were arranged with designated areas to accommodate learning through sight, sound, and touch. Every subject's curricula were adapted to meet the needs of left- and right-brain processing, including tools for multisensory teaching.

We can learn a lot from the emphasis our schools place on holistic learning. As I began studying this area, it felt as though I was entering a whole new world—one left largely unexplored by the church. And in the process, I found two approaches to identifying the ways in which we learn:

Type of Learner: How we interact with information

Type of Thinker: How we process information

I prefer to use the word *type* over the word *style* because I believe that the way we learn is more of an inherent characteristic than a preference.

TYPES OF LEARNERS

We receive information through our senses and, generally, the more senses we involve in any learning experience, the better we'll retain the information. However, each of us has a proclivity toward certain sensory learning modes. If we're not given the opportunity to use those senses, then we tend to "switch off" and are far less likely to learn effectively.[1]

Most of us are predominantly one type of learner; but, depending on the environment, we may adapt to other types. The three most common types are:

VISUAL LEARNERS

- Process information by watching
- Identify images to relate to an experience
- Respond well to images, graphics, symbols, diagrams, key words, and demonstrations

AUDITORY LEARNERS

- Process information by hearing
- Identify sounds to relate to an experience
- Respond well to spoken words, discussion, music, and poems

PHYSICAL (KINESTHETIC) LEARNERS

- Process information by touch and movement
- Identify feelings to relate to an experience
- Respond well to written assignments, object lessons, field trips, and participation

TYPES OF THINKERS

Thinking type differs from learning type in that it has more to do with how we cognitively process information than how our senses interact with it. As with learning types, most people are predisposed (but not limited) to one of these types, but some people function well using two or three types.

Education gurus Peter Honey and Alan Mumford identified four different types of thinkers: Reflective (Analytic), Creative (Active), Practical (Pragmatic), and Conceptual (Theorist).[2] I've adapted the descriptions of these types to bring some additional clarity and usefulness.

REFLECTIVE (ANALYTIC) THINKERS

- Analytical and careful
- Prefer to keep a low profile
- View new information subjectively
- Take time to ponder and make observations
- Relate new information to past experiences
- Examine their feelings about what they're learning
- Don't like to be rushed to make quick decisions

PRACTICAL (PRAGMATIC) THINKERS

- Seek the simplest, most efficient way
- Prefer to act quickly and get impatient with process
- Desire immediate relevance
- Not satisfied without specific applications and directions
- Want factual information
- Accept new information only after seeing the big picture

CREATIVE (ACTIVE) THINKERS

- Imaginative, enthusiastic, and open-ended
- Prefer activity and attention
- Make excellent troubleshooters
- Create their own solutions and shortcuts
- Tend to get bored easily, dislike repetition
- Learn well from reading and synthesizing information

CONCEPTUAL (THEORIST) THINKERS

- Value rationality and logic above all
- Prefer to analyze and synthesize
- Want to know how things work and learn related concepts
- Can be detached from their emotions
- Uncomfortable with subjectivity and ambiguity
- Like to be intellectually stretched

LEARNING CONNECTIONS

As we explore types of learning and thought, we can only assume that we—and our students—will connect more and assume a more active role at different segments of the storying process. I'm a visual learner, so I was concerned that storying wouldn't connect with my need to "see it." However, I learned that stories have the ability to draw in any learning type because of their imaginative nature.

Storying is a perfect tool for meeting the needs of different types of learners. It involves participants right from the start and through a variety of learning methods—storytelling, visualizing, dialogue, retelling, creative activities...you name it.

STORYING SEGMENT	LEARNING CONNECTION (**BOLD** indicates whom it connects the best with)
REVIEW	• **Visual Learners—connects with their "mental timeline"** • Auditory Learners—contributing/processing thoughts out loud • Physical Learners—artistic mediums and participation
	• **Reflective Thinkers—like to relate information to past experiences** • Creative Thinkers—like creative and imaginative dynamics • Practical Thinkers—get to replay facts of previous stories • Conceptual Thinkers—see how stories interrelate
STORYTELLING	• Visual Learners—vivid descriptions spark mental imagery • **Auditory Learners—vivid audible descriptions** • Physical Learners—take notes to follow along
	• Reflective Thinkers—connect with emotion of story, good listeners • **Creative Thinkers—like creative and imaginative dynamics** • Practical Thinkers—emphasis on big picture and details • Conceptual Thinkers—emphasis on big picture and ideas
RETELLING	• Visual Learners—reenactments and artistic mediums • Auditory Learners—processing thoughts out loud • **Physical Learners—artistic mediums and participation**
	• **Reflective Thinkers—will focus on the details and the emotion of the story** • Creative Thinkers—like creative and imaginative dynamics • Practical Thinkers—get to replay facts of stories • Conceptual Thinkers—connect with the linear events of the story

STORYING SEGMENT	LEARNING CONNECTION (BOLD indicates whom it connects the best with)
DIALOGUE	• Visual Learners—like imaginative questions • **Auditory Learners—processing thoughts out loud** • Physical Learners—participation in a discussion
	• Reflective Thinkers—create a safe place to process information • Creative Thinkers—enjoy interaction and participation, imaginative questions • Practical Thinkers—make connections to details and themes in stories • **Conceptual Thinkers—can share theories and synthesis**
CONNECTION	• Visual Learners—make connections between the stories, artistic expression • Auditory Learners—processing thoughts out loud • **Physical Learners—participation in a discussion, writing, prayer**
	• Reflective Thinkers—creates a safe place to process, connects with feelings • Creative Thinkers—enjoy interaction and participation, problem solving • **Practical Thinkers—desire application and relevance** • Conceptual Thinkers—like closure and will challenge group to dream big

STORYING FOLLOWS THE EXPERIENTIAL LEARNING CYCLE

Learning is rooted in *experiencing* the information, not the information itself. Education pioneer John Dewey said, "There is an intimate and necessary relation between the processes of actual experience and education."[3] Dewey's writing and educational philosophy is the basis of many Western theories of education and largely shaped the Experiential Learning Cycle.

**Tell me and I will forget.
Show me, and I may remember.
Involve me, and I will understand.
—Confucius, 450 BC**

Developed by David Kolb in 1984, the Experiential Learning Cycle is the most widely used and accepted model describing the application of learning in education. The heart of Kolb's model proposes four stages that move us toward applied learning.[4] I've adapted the descriptions of these stages to offer some additional clarity and usefulness. I've also overlaid the segments of the storying process onto the diagram so you can see how it follows the Experiential Learning Cycle.

Kolb's model isn't just informative; it's also a helpful tool for evaluation. We can examine our ministries in light of this cycle, assessing if we're balanced in providing learning opportunities in each stage. Investing in each stage of the cycle is critical, as the stages are interdependent and build upon each other. And each stage contributes to forming a foundation for subsequent learning.

For example, one youth worker's Tuesday-night small group regularly skims over the Review/Observation stage, spending little time looking in depth at background and content of the Bible passage being studied. The leader says, "We like to get right to the application discussion and answer the question, 'What does this mean for us?'" As a result, the group seems impatient with background information and struggles to value the Bible's content. (I've been there!) This Bible study contributes to its members' lack of foundation for learning based on the Scriptures. This seems to be a big problem in many churches in America.

It's essential for us to follow the entire cycle in order to facilitate effective learning. Students who experience this process on a regular basis will appreciate the opportunity to engage in ways that fit them, build self-confidence, share more frequently, and be more open to try new things.

As teachers, we gravitate toward particular segments of the learning cycle. I know I could spend all day in the Process/Connecting segment—I love asking questions and letting ideas circulate! The danger in doing this is if time is short, then we'll tend to focus only on our favorite parts of the cycle, cutting short the rest. If we don't want to exclude some of our students from developing to their full potential, then we must practice giving equal weight to every part of the cycle.[5]

The great thing is that the process of storying works well within the Experiential Learning Cycle. Storying calls us to facilitate an experience of the Bible that helps participants develop as learners, growing their skills to discover and create as an act of worship to God.

A LEARNER-CENTERED FOCUS

As we begin to study the most effective methods of helping others learn, we discover that moving from teacher/lecture-based to learner-based methods is imperative. Years of research have shown that motivation, learning, and success are enhanced when learner-centered principles and practices are in place. Throughout North America, educational institutions on all levels have transitioned to a learner-centered philosophy of teaching.

Storying is designed as learner-centered teaching. To effectively lead the storying process will require all of us to adopt new methods, to let go of some of the control we're used to having, to seek patience, and to trust the Holy Spirit to speak to and through a community of young learners.

Maryellen Weimer, author of *Learner-Centered Teaching*, says that in order for teaching to more effectively promote learning, our thinking and practices need to change in five areas:

A TRUE STORY ABOUT STORYING

I grew up cultured in story. From movies to my friends' fables of their past experiences, I was consumed with a narrative. But it took a little while to figure out that stories are a large part of Scripture. I interned under Michael Novelli for my undergraduate work in youth ministry. He loved this "new" concept and talked about it and how it adds so much depth to our understanding of the Scriptures, as well as our relationship to them. I slowly caught on, and I, too, have seen the impact of storying, both personally and in my ministry.

The year following my time with Michael, my friend Joe and I were asked to start up a youth program for a local church. As Joe and I discussed our thoughts and convictions about what this new ministry could be, I was quick to suggest the element of storying. So for the first year, Joe and I tried to build relationships with the students. And during our Sunday evening gatherings, we'd come together for a story. It started slowly—the concept seemed elementary to most of the students (and parents and volunteers). Joe and I, however, stuck it out; and since then, we've begun to see something beautiful emerge.

My students who had little to no Bible knowledge were starting to get it; they began entering into and making connections with the stories to see the redemptive rainbow that unites the Scriptures.

Seeing Scripture as God's Story became an annual rhythm of our year. The students started creating art and relating it to Scripture. Each week would be something different. For instance, when we participated in the story of creation, the students had to create with clay something that represented the human condition. Most of them created something that represented the idea of wholeness, connectedness with the Godhead, happiness. When we went into the rebellion of mankind, they were asked to create something that represented the state of humanity with sin in the picture. In the youth room, we maintained an open wall for student art—a place to display the students' masterpieces about the stories.

Storying helped our students become more knowledgeable about Scripture and its narrative of redemption and restoration. It also gave them a more complete view of the Bible.

—CHRIS STEWART, YOUTH WORKER IN ELGIN, ILLINOIS

1. THE ROLE OF THE TEACHER

We move into a role of coaching and mentoring students to facilitate their own learning, designing experiences through which students acquire new knowledge and develop new skills. The goal of all teachers should be enabling students to be lifelong learners and giving them tools to succeed in this venture.

2. THE BALANCE OF POWER

The effectiveness of learner-centered methods depends on teachers being able to step aside and let students take the lead. However, having been at the center for so long, we may find it tough to leave that spot, even briefly.

3. THE FUNCTION OF CONTENT

The underlying philosophy is that students learn best not only by receiving knowledge, but also by interpreting it, learning through discovery, and setting the pace for their own learning.

4. THE RESPONSIBILITY FOR LEARNING

We need to shift responsibility for learning to the students. The primary goal of a teacher is to create a "climate for learning." Don't underestimate your power to model a passion for learning.

5. THE PURPOSE AND PROCESSES OF EVALUATION

In this model, evaluation and purposes shift. It becomes less about students taking away our specific applications and more about a myriad of implications as they involve themselves in teaching and learning from each other. This method of learning is messy—a lot more like real life!

BECOME AN EXPERIENCE ARCHITECT

One of the defining words for this digital era is *interactive*. We're becoming accustomed to being able to access and create our own media at a moment's notice. We desire to contribute to our own learning and entertainment like we would any conversation. We now yearn to be a part of shared experience.

This shift in values has significant implications for the way we approach education. Places where we've traditionally accessed information—schools, libraries, and museums—have identified this shift and moved to making their learning opportunities more interactive. There is a new set of standards for how we teach others. We are moving away from one-dimensional education with the teachers being the experts who hold the key to information.

Students already have instant access to most information. They're becoming accustomed to being able to change, interact, and create while they learn.

We teachers and leaders then become guides to help students explore information and use it in the right context. This requires a new vision for our roles as educators. We become "experience architects," creating environments that help participants dive deeper and explore further into the things of God. This new role requires a significant investment of energy into creativity.

Storying will help you explore your new role as an experience architect. The storying process encourages you to experiment with all kinds of creative exercises that will foster learning and formation in your students.

QUESTIONS FOR RESPONSE AND DISCUSSION

Which parts of this chapter did you relate to your own story?

What type of learner are you? What type of thinker are you?

What learning environments/methods have you connected with the best?

What part of the Experiential Learning Cycle energizes you? What part is most challenging for you to engage with?

Do you believe it's important for ministries to embrace learner-centered methods? Why?

What are some ways you could make your ministry more learner-centered?

NOTES

1. Sue Price, "The Learning Cycle: A Pattern for Learning," extract from *Children's Ministry Guide to Tailored Teaching for 5-9s*, Children's Ministry Web page, http://www.childrensministry.co.uk/teaching-programme/reaching-each-you-teach/article_index.php?id=69 (accessed May 15, 2008).

2. Peter Honey and Alan Mumford, *The Manual of Learning Styles* (Berkshire, UK: Peter Honey Publications, 1982).

3. John Dewey, *Experience and Education* (New York: Simon & Schuster, 1938), 20.

4. David A. Kolb, *Experiential Learning: Experience as the Source of Learning and Development* (Upper Saddle River, NJ: Prentice Hall, 1984).

5. Price, "The Learning Cycle: A Pattern for Learning."

STORYING AND FORMATION
CHAPTER 9

The purpose of the Experiential Learning Cycle is to move participants to "applied learning" (in other words, learning that invokes changes in thought and behavior). Educators use the term *development* to describe these changes, while we in the church use the term *formation*. In this context, both terms describe the same idea—**internal shaping and growth that leads toward outward action.** The term *transformation* means to complete a change from one form to another. And *conversion* is a type of transformation.

Discipleship involves more than a transfer of information (informative); it's a relationship that involves being shaped by God, God's Story, and others' stories—it is formation (formative).[1] Experiencing the Bible as story is a catalyst for transformation. God inhabits his story, illuminating it to us, drawing us into it, and reshaping our perspective. Through the Story, God gives us new eyes, and it begins to permeate and reorder all areas of our lives.

Preben Vang and Terry Carter describe the transformative power of God's Story in their book *Telling God's Story*:

> Our lives as human beings are made up of stories that have shaped, or are shaping, who we are. The story of the Bible has the power to make sense of all the other stories of your life. When it is internalized and it becomes your story, it gives meaning in the midst of meaninglessness and value in the midst of worthlessness. Your personal story will find grounding in creation, guidance in crises, re-formation in redemption, and direction in its destination. People become Christians when their own stories merge with, and are understood in the light of, God's story.[2]

STAGES OF FORMATION

This graphic may help provide more clarity to how formation takes place through story:

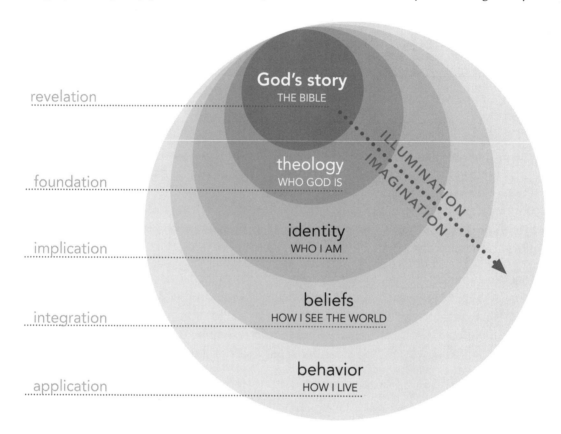

(Thanks to my colleague Chris Folmsbee for helping develop some of the wording for this graphic.)

REVELATION—GOD'S STORY (THE BIBLE)

The Bible story must be the starting point and centerpiece of our learning as followers of Jesus. While this may seem obvious, most often we focus on *ideas* from the Bible. With God's Story as the emphasis, Scripture becomes a guiding voice for us to follow and a vital, living member of our community for us to listen and respond to.

In *The God-Hungry Imagination,* Sarah Arthur writes:

> Without past or future, it is tough to find meaning in the present…Story is the primary way we impart what really matters to the next generation. Stories have the potential to embody biblical and theological content in ways that sink into the imagination, take root, and grow.[3]

For years I didn't know how to make the Bible the center of my ministry. I focused on different points, wondering why students weren't applying what I taught them.

MY MINISTRY FOCAL POINTS	MY DESIRED OUTCOME FOR STUDENTS
Topic-based studies and messages	How to live and behave like a Christian
Serving and mission trip experiences	Challenge worldview/perspective
Spiritual formation experiences *(labyrinths, journaling, prayer)*	Create space to discover God
Leadership training	Share faith and embrace a new calling
Games and activities	Address identity as part of a community
Systematic theology *(attributes of God, books of the Bible, Jesus' life and teachings)*	Shape students' understanding of God
Inductive Bible study	Let Scripture reveal God to students

Most of us would agree that emphasizing these things can be good. However, I'd like to suggest that none of these focal points serves as a good starting place. When we emphasize HOW we want people to live, without providing a deep vision for WHY, we risk focusing on little more than behavior modification. *We're motivating people to live for a story that isn't their own.* Thus, they have no connection to or context for the greater Story.

> **Each of us has a canon of sacred stories. Those stories help form what we believe to be true about the world now, and will largely determine what we believe about the future. We cannot fundamentally change ourselves without changing our stories.**
>
> **—DANIEL TAYLOR, *TELL ME A STORY: THE LIFE-SHAPING POWER OF OUR STORIES***

When I was in high school, I genuinely lived like a Christian because I was told that's what I should do. My motivation was based on what I (and many of us) had been taught—something I call "eternal payback": i.e., *Jesus loves you and sacrificed his life for you, so you should do the same for him.* That made sense, but it felt more like a transaction than a relationship. At times I felt emotionally connected to this decision, but I never really understood the idea of my "owing" God.

Internally, my real motivation was *acceptance*—I wanted to please my youth leader and fit into our youth group. It wasn't because my identity had changed or I had a really deep encounter with God. I didn't even realize what my motivations were at the time. In my mind, I was sincere in my Christianity.

How many of our students have embraced their identities and calling as God's own? I fear that most don't even know *why* they're supposed to live for God because we've focused so much on *how* we expect them to live. We've provided only limited views and shallow pictures of the kingdom of God in which we're called to live.

We must help our students understand that following Jesus is more than just "eternal payback." Our focus should be to help others find themselves in God's Story—discovering who God is and who God created them to be. *We're called to give others a better story.*

FOUNDATION—THEOLOGY (WHO GOD IS)

When our focus and starting point is God's Story, theology is the first area that's shaped. I use the word *theology* in a simple sense here, describing our understanding of the character and nature of God. (I'm not referring to *theology* in the academic and systematic sense.)

When we approach the Bible as story, right away it becomes clear that the story is foremost about God, and all kinds of images about God's nature unfold before us. I believe the primary function of the Bible is to reveal to us what God is like and what God desires for the world. As one of my students put it, "The stories showed me God's character and how the Bible fits together...how all of the stories point to Jesus!"

The beauty of story is that it stretches our imaginations...it begins to give us a sense of the bigness of God in ways we've never seen before.

Story also lays a framework for all of our Bible learning. It gives us a mental timeline of the Story, which is a foundation for future understanding. When we hear a sermon or read a passage, we can then put it into the context of the bigger story.

> "Aslan," said Lucy, "you're bigger."
> "That is because you are older, little one," answered he.
> "Not because you are?"
> "I am not. But every year you grow, you will find me bigger."
>
> *—PRINCE CASPIAN* BY C. S. LEWIS

"Narrative becomes a hopeful way for people to regain a hearing of the theological voice in Scriptures." —George W. Stroup, *The Promise of Narrative Theology*

IMPLICATION—IDENTITY AND CALLING (WHO I AM)

When approached as narrative, the Bible Story has a subtle way of getting into our heads and under our skin. At first it seems nonintrusive because it's a faraway story about a distant people. But then it begins to work on us...the messages beneath the surface emerge, and we're captivated by its story. We find ourselves inside that story, identifying and empathizing with the characters. It becomes part of our experience and identity—*it is now our story.*

This is called *implication*, which has a much different meaning from *application*. Many of us have been trained to think, *How does the Bible apply to me?* Yet, *application* literally means "to put on the surface." Thus, like a Band-Aid or salve, we try to administer the Scriptures to our own situations.

To be *implicated* is to be bound with, wrapped up, and twisted together like the strands of a rope. The word *implicate* comes from the Latin word meaning "folded in." We become intertwined and folded in to God's Story, and it speaks to and informs us as to who we are and why we're here.

So our question moves from "How do I apply this to my situation?" to "What does this mean for the way I live my life?" We begin to seek our role in the story, rather than try to figure out what to do with it.

Implication calls us *toward* something—to redefine what we know, to a new way of life lived with our community of faith. God's Story cultivates hope within us. We begin to envision how we can change our community, our world, and ourselves.

A sophomore girl in my youth group put it this way: "These stories showed me that God gave us a purpose in life—to live for him and not ourselves." A senior guy saw it this way: "It made me realize...I need to live for the Author. He has a story for my life that I'm excited to discover, and I want to share with others. His amazing Story is what we've been waiting for our entire lives..."

INTEGRATION—CONVICTIONS AND BELIEFS (HOW I THINK AND SEE)

After the story permeates our theology and identity, it then begins to shape our convictions and beliefs. It moves beyond just forming how we see God and ourselves to how we see our world.

God's Spirit gives us new eyes to see life through a different lens—a supernatural perspective informed by the Story to show us how to live in the ways of God. God's Story begins to replace our own stories and agendas as our lives are rebuilt around a new Story. We're empowered to "put on the new self, which is being renewed in knowledge in the image of its Creator" (Colossians 3:10 NIV).

A TRUE STORY ABOUT STORYING

This past year our youth ministry spent 22 weeks making our way through the Story of God. Each episode brought to life stories that my students had heard since they were kids but had never seen as being applicable to their lives.

When we first began, the main comment the leaders heard was, "We've heard these stories before." But as the students wrestled with the stories, they soon realized they didn't know the stories as well as they thought they did. They found a freedom to ask questions they'd always been too afraid to ask in Sunday school, fearing they'd stump the teacher.

God did some amazing things in those weeks. Two students came to know Christ as a result of the Story of God. We also had many new believers who couldn't get enough. Students who'd been Christians for years were being challenged in new ways and by stories they'd heard for years.

As a result, the students in our ministry have really taken ownership of God's Story. They now see the big picture of how God demonstrated his love for mankind and restored our relationship to him. My students also understand that they're a continuation of that Story. On the last night, we had an empty canvas displayed at the front of the room. I challenged the students to come up and write about how they'd continue the Story. Their comments were amazing, and that canvas now hangs in our youth room as a reminder of our commitment.

The Story of God has made a profound impact on my ministry. It's laid a foundation that I can now build on. It's so encouraging to see how the students are now able to fit our weekly lessons into the big picture of God's Story.

—DAVE LANE, YOUTH WORKER IN SARNIA, ONTARIO

Our perspective on everything changes—we're invited to live in a different reality. God's Spirit opens our imaginations, and a new worldview is woven into the fabric of who we are. Eventually, our new identities are integrated into our everyday lives.

A high school senior shared with my group, "Through the stories, I got a picture of how I should and shouldn't live. I related to the struggles of the Israelites, and I saw how much I need God." A sophomore revealed, "I'm learning more than ever before. I saw that I really wasn't a believer. The stories pulled me back in."

APPLICATION—BEHAVIOR AND PRACTICES (HOW I LIVE)

When our theology, identity, and beliefs are shaped by God's Story, we're motivated to take action on what we believe about God, ourselves, and our world. Our behavior is informed by the Story. We aren't just grasping for an application; we have a context and a deep foundation to make godly decisions.

Story helps our application move beyond good decision making and right living to envision our role in God's activity in the world. The story ignites our imaginations to become co-creators with God, expressing itself in many ways: Serving, prayer, the arts, hospitality, truth telling—the possibilities are endless.

The amazing thing is that application becomes implicit...the Story informs our experiences and shapes how we should live. This happens without us teachers having to hand out a list of application points. We're moved toward restorative action.

One student shared, "I feel that I need to live like I want to be part of God's Story." Another noticed, "I saw real life being applied to God's Story...I thought about how I'm like the characters in God's Story."

"Aren't we supposed to be God's blessing to others, like Abraham?" a student from my youth group asked. "Well, my brother and I have a couple of ideas about this..." This student went on to initiate opportunities for our group to regularly serve meals to the homeless, and he also led an outreach for students at his school. All of this because he saw himself as a continuation of God's Story. I was really encouraged when this same student decided to change his college plans so he could pursue youth ministry.

Garrett Green describes the Story's role in formation this way: "Being conformed to this image means shaping one's life after Christ's life, patterning one's own living according to the pattern of his story, following the example of Jesus. The *imago Dei* [image of God] is thus restored, not as some kind of spiritual substance ('soul') but in the 'narrative shape' of the Christian life."[4]

God's Story is what gives shape and context to our lives as we follow in the ways of Jesus. May we allow it to speak, inform, and reorder our lives so we may discover our role in God's kingdom.

QUESTIONS FOR RESPONSE AND DISCUSSION

Which parts of this chapter did you relate to your own story?

How do you believe stories shape who we are?

How has God's Story shaped your life?

How do ministries sometimes emphasize behavior modification instead of formation?

NOTES

1. Sarah Arthur, *The God-Hungry Imagination: The Art of Storytelling for Postmodern Youth Ministry* (Nashville, Tenn.: Upper Room Books, 2007), 28.
2. Preben Vang and Terry Carter, *Telling God's Story: The Biblical Narrative from Beginning to End* (Nashville, Tenn.: Broadman & Holman, 2006), 9.
3. Arthur, 17.
4. Garrett Green, *Imagining God: Theology and the Religious Imagination* (San Francisco: HarperCollins, 1989), 101.

STORYING ESSENTIALS
CHAPTER 10

SETTINGS FOR STORYING

Storying is effective in a variety of settings: Weekend retreats, weekly studies, weeklong camps, and so on. I've had the opportunity to lead storying in all of these settings, and they all have advantages and challenges. The best settings are those in which ample time is allowed for the storying process.

The most challenging (and least effective) use of storying has been when I tried to cover a lot of stories in a short amount of time. I've had numerous opportunities when I was asked to cover the entire biblical storyline in two days or less. To do that well, you have to cover 12 to 15 narratives at a minimum. As interactive as storying is, telling that many stories in that short a time feels like information overload.

Weekly studies and weeklong events are better settings for storying than retreats. I've helped create a weeklong interactive event called Merge that takes students through 15 key narratives in God's Story. (For more information go to www.mergeevent.com. Should you need some guidance while planning how to utilize storying in your setting, I would love to help. You can email me at michael@echothestory.com.)

The remainder of this section will focus on the elements within a storying session.

CREATING AN ENVIRONMENT FOR STORYING

In almost any culture, the most personal place of communication is at our dining tables, especially around a meal. Meeting there speaks of relationship, equality, and family. That is the hope of storying: *To create a safe place for us to share openly, be encouraged, and feel loved.*

That doesn't necessarily mean you have to sit around a table—but it would be great if you could! You should try to sit in a circle where everyone can make eye contact and hear each other well. Do everything you can to create a place where each person feels like an equal.

We moved our group from meeting in the youth room at the church to meeting in a home—away from all of the games and hip atmosphere. I wanted our students to see that youth group was not a program to attend, but rather a community—a family—that we can be a part of. About 18 of us would sit in a circle in the living room of one of our students' houses. Sometimes I'd light a candle to symbolize the beginning of the storytelling.

With my students, I rarely use any technology. The "media" I use the most are markers and paper. I do this intentionally, so together we can create any of the visuals used in storying. This is not to say that technology can't be helpful. However, I was concerned it would be more of a distraction than a vehicle to help build imagination and listening. I wanted to "shock the system" of what my students were used to and go low-tech.

I used to sit on a stool and use a music stand for my notes when I told the stories. After thinking about this for a while, I realized that those items differentiate me from the rest of the group—literally setting me above them. *So I got rid of them.* It wasn't that big of a deal for me to sit in a chair and hold my notes. I want the group to know that I'm a colearner and a full participant in learning from God's Story.

We're already fighting the notion that only experts have something meaningful to say about the Bible. Students are used to hearing the "right answers." We must do all we can to remove any obstacles that may hinder our students from sharing.

I understand that many of our meeting spaces present some unique challenges. For instance, some of us have large groups, and we have to get creative to figure out how to create safe places for open dialogue.

The environment you create communicates a lot. If we meet in a room where one person stands on stage with a spotlight and a microphone and the rest of the group sits facing that person, then what might that communicate? To me, it communicates that I'm not expected to participate, but spectate. This is the opposite of the environment we should strive to create.

STORYING WITH LARGER GROUPS

Storying is designed to allow everyone time to share observations about the story. This creates some challenges when working with larger groups. Over the last several years I've been "experimenting" with different ways to create environments for storying with larger groups. If you're planning on implementing this approach in a large group, I would love to brainstorm with you some creative solutions.

In planning our Merge Student events, we faced a lot of challenges as we tried to figure out how to do storying and interactive experiences with hundreds of students all at once. We created several group-led experiences and walkthrough activities (e.g., a tabernacle for students to learn about by entering). We even did a Passover Seder with the entire group! Those activities took careful planning and extra creativity.

As a general guideline, **if I have more than 25 participants, I'll divide them into smaller groups.** This is essential to allow time and opportunity for everyone to share. The following are some approaches to structuring storying for large groups that I've found effective:

LARGE GROUP STORYTELLING, SMALL GROUP DIALOGUE

Many of the larger groups I've worked with lead storytelling with the entire group together then break into small groups for the retelling and dialogue. Then trained adult leaders facilitate the small group dialogues. This approach to storying works well—in fact, it's the same approach we've taken with our Merge student events. The challenge is finding and training good volunteer dialogue leaders. (Should you need help, this is my specialty—I spend a lot of time working with churches to help train volunteers to lead storying groups.)

PREPARING YOUR GROUP FOR STORYING

Before you begin storying with your group, plan an activity to help them think about their favorite stories and what makes them so engaging. It could be as simple as discussing your own favorite stories or viewing a clip from a movie with a powerful story and discussing it.

My friend Seth showed a short segment from the middle of one of the *Lord of the Rings* movies. Then he asked his students to describe the events that led up to that scene. Seth made the point that we need to know the entire story—from the beginning—in order to really understand each scene.

A TYPICAL STORYING SESSION

The following is a storying format that I've used with students many times. Ideally, it should be used in a time slot when you have at least two hours or more to meet. And this outline isn't set in stone—there are many ways you can approach storying. What's important is that you allow enough time so you're not hurrying through the process.

In this chapter, I'll go into greater depth about the elements 1 through 5.

ELEMENT	ESTIMATED TIME
1. BUILD community	30 minutes
2. REVIEW previous stories	15-20 minutes
3. PREPARE for imaginative listening	2 minutes
4. NARRATE the new story	10 minutes
5. Help the group RETELL the new story	20 minutes
6. DIALOGUE (discussion) about the story	40-45 minutes
7. CONNECT the story to our own stories	10 minutes
(Ideas for these elements are in Appendix B.)	

STORYING SESSION ELEMENTS

1. BUILD COMMUNITY

Have a meal together, play a game, and connect relationally. Don't underestimate the power of laughter and fun.

2. REVIEW PREVIOUS STORIES

Review should be fast-paced and fun. Review is especially important if you're doing storying in a weekly format. The goal in reviewing past stories is to help the group make connections between the stories and see how each story fits into a larger narrative. Spend additional time reviewing the story from the previous session to get everyone up to speed.

I'd also encourage you to plan one or two sessions that solely focus on review. These are important points for your group to be able to look back, remember, and think about what they're learning from the stories as a whole.

I've used symbols during the review time, asking participants to draw them or identify the story that goes with each of them. My symbols are intentionally simple so anyone can draw and remember them (see below). You may even want to see if your group can come up with their own symbols. Have fun with this and be creative. (For some additional ideas, see the Retelling pages in Appendix B.)

Review example: "Can anyone tell me—in 30 seconds or less—what happened in our last story?" Get one or two students to give you a quick overview. Draw the symbols for the stories you've already covered. You may want to ask a student volunteer to draw these symbols each time.

3. PREPARE FOR IMAGINATIVE LISTENING

Your group will come to each meeting with a certain level of personal distraction—tiredness, stress, hyperactivity, and so on. The storying process is very repetitive, and some students who are accustomed to constant stimulation from media and video games tend to lose focus easily. You'll need to be intentional in helping them refocus *every session* and coaching them to be attentive listeners.

Your storytelling time needs to take a different tone from the rest of your group time—a slower, more focused pace. You'll need to set the tone for this, letting students know that it's a special time and they'll need to work hard at concentrating and getting into "storying mode." To help them get started, you may want to light a candle to signify storying as a holy practice.

Make sure you tell participants that there's to be no talking during the storytelling. They should plan to find a focal point in the room to look at, close their eyes, or take notes—whatever will help them focus completely on the story. Encourage your group to further engage through imaginative listening. *Imaginative listening* is simply using your imagination to picture the story in your mind—like you would a movie—and imagine that you're in the scene.

> "We humans are sight mammals. We learn almost twice as well from images and words as from words alone. Visual language engages both hemispheres of the brain. Pictures translate across cultures, education levels, and age groups."[1]

Let your group know that they'll also be part of a retelling and discussion time during which you'll ask them what details they noticed in the story. This often helps improve the students' attentiveness because they know they'll probably be called upon.

Right before you begin telling the story, take a quiet moment to slow down and allow participants to clear their minds, close their eyes, and whisper a prayer asking God to speak to them through the story.

Remember, repetition is good. So plan to refocus your group every time you meet. It may seem redundant to you, but trust me—the more you help them focus and encourage them to pay attention, the greater their participation and engagement.

I've provided some specific opener ideas for you to use (see Appendix B). Make sure you read through them. Even better—tweak them and make them your own.

4. NARRATE THE NEW STORY

Your role is not just reading words off a page, but bringing those words to life. Storytelling is more like the work of an artist than that of a teacher. It's less about explaining and more about exploring. Our role is to help each other participate in the stories of God. As we participate in these stories, they become our own—the gospel happens to us.

PREPARE FOR STORYTELLING

Live with the story. Spend time in the story until the characters and setting become visual to you. Picture them in your mind, imagining the sounds, tastes, scents, and colors. Slow down and enjoy it as you read through the story several times.

Know the story. If you are a visual learner, read the narrative over and over. Draw a "storyboard" as if you were going to create a movie, with boxes for each of the key events. If you are an auditory learner, the more you read the story aloud the more you will connect with it. Record it and play it back for yourself. If you are a kinesthetic (physical) learner, stand and act out parts of the story as you tell it.

Listen to some audio stories. To help you prepare, you can download audio versions of my narratives at www.echothestory.com. These audios are intended to help you prepare, not replace you as the storyteller. You can do it! Have confidence and know that imparting these stories to your group is an important relational act.

A TRUE STORY ABOUT STORYING

A few years ago, I had the opportunity to train at a student ministry conference with Michael Novelli. Throughout the conference we used his storying process and a biblical story set that he'd written. This was my first exposure to the art of storying and the process really brought a lot of things together in my understanding of the Bible and ministry. As I worked with Michael, I witnessed firsthand the amazing way that God's Story reshapes students into his image. As a middle school pastor, I was inspired by Michael's vision.

On the surface, it's such a basic idea that it seems unlikely to succeed. But as many have pointed out, we truly live in a culture that no longer knows the Story of God. I know this is true of the students I work with. Some know a few pieces or favorite parts of the story, but almost no one knows the overarching story that connects all of life together. A lot of student curricula focus on either morality or God trivia. While those who do so *mean* well, it often results in a fragmented understanding of God and an inability to grasp the worldview of the Word.

Once I was exposed to storying, I was hooked. Our youth group immediately began using chronological storying. Over the course of a year, we worked through the Old Testament, working hard to help students see the overarching story. By using the storytelling and review techniques that I'd first observed Michael using, our students were able to grasp the flow and significance of the Old Testament in a new way. Students not only got it, but they also remembered the stories from week to week and really got into the retelling of them. As the weeks went on, they also began to grasp what the stories meant in their lives.

Now I'm working with the same students through a second year of storying. We're in the middle of the New Testament, and they still remember the stories that got us here. It's clear that not only are they getting the story, but it's also getting inside of them in cool ways. They're making real connections between the events of God's Story and their daily lives. I believe they're beginning to see that there really is only one story—and they're in it.

—BRANDON BROWN, YOUTH WORKER IN MILWAUKEE, WISCONSIN

Work through a story observation exercise. This exercise is designed to help you think deeply about a story before you tell it. It can be completed alone or in a group. As we look carefully at stories, we must think more in terms of events than outlines. Most stories are a sequence of events involving character, setting, action, conflict, climax, and resolution.

Read the following Scripture passage slowly three times. Between readings, write down your observations by answering the questions outlined for each.

> As evening came, Jesus said to his disciples, "Let's cross to the other side of the lake." So they took Jesus in the boat and started out, leaving the crowds behind (although other boats followed). But soon a fierce storm came up. High waves were breaking into the boat, and it began to fill with water.
>
> Jesus was sleeping at the back of the boat with his head on a cushion. The disciples woke him up, shouting, "Teacher, don't you care that we're going to drown?"
>
> When Jesus woke up, he rebuked the wind and said to the waves, "Silence! Be still!" Suddenly the wind stopped, and there was a great calm. Then he asked them, "Why are you afraid? Do you still have no faith?"
>
> The disciples were absolutely terrified. "Who is this man?" they asked each other. "Even the wind and waves obey him!" —Mark 4:35-41 (NLT)

First Reading—Any Questions?

- Is there anything you don't understand?
- Is there anything that surprises you?
- Is there anything that piques your curiosity?
- Is there anything that strikes you as significant?

Second Reading—Plot Development

- What are the main events of this story? List the events in order.
- Where is tension building and what problems arise?
- Where is the high point in the action? Where is the climax?
- How did the story end? Were the tensions resolved? How?

Draw a story map (line chart) like this one:

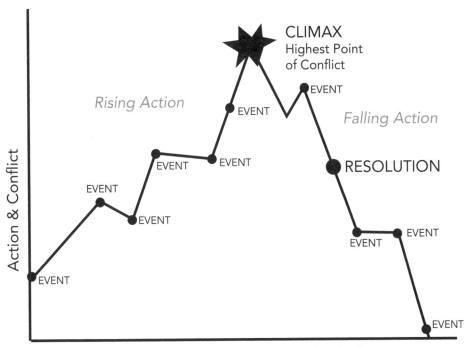

Identify the main events, conflict points, climax, resolution, and conclusion of the story on your chart.

Third Reading—Character Development

- Were any phrases repeated in the story?
- Where does the story take place? What is the culture like?
- List the main characters and describe character traits of each from this story—their words, deeds, strengths, and weaknesses.
- What emotions were expressed, if any, by each character?
- Which characters do you identify with the most? Why?

STORYTELLING ESSENTIALS

Stick to the story. Strive to be as accurate as possible in your telling. Don't mix in other elements from your knowledge of future stories. The narratives I've provided are already condensed. Skipping parts of them can leave out key elements that connect with future stories and can mess up the dialogue time.

Tell the story from beginning to end—don't stop! Stopping to answer a question, teach, clarify, give application, or make an observation causes confusion. Save it for the dialogue time.

Speak simply and clearly. Don't add lots of words—we have a tendency to try to be more descriptive and detailed than the text. Don't. Good storytellers use fewer words and shorter sentences, and they also allow space for their listeners to imagine.

Be genuinely animated and enthusiastic! Use gestures and facial expressions—but be sure they're appropriate and natural. You need to BRING ENERGY to this process.

Avoid joking and sarcasm. They can project a very different meaning from the biblical meaning you believe you're projecting.

Be aware of your pacing. Pacing involves both the volume and rate at which you speak and the progression of the action in the story. Dialogue slows a story's pace, while narrating action speeds it up.

Repeat. Repeat. Repeat. Repetition has always been a basic element of storytelling—don't fear it just because it's not as common in other forms of teaching.

Be humble. Tell stories with servanthood and sincerity—remember that we're privileged to tell God's Story.

Be patient with the process. At first, some in your group may believe this process is too basic. After you're a few stories into it, they'll realize how much there is to be learned and get into the rhythm of this different approach to teaching.

Relax and be yourself. Develop your own style—one that you're comfortable with.

A TRUE STORY ABOUT STORYING

We decided to use storying for our junior and senior high small groups. We did a training day on our own, and then we allowed the leaders to use the material for a couple of small groups. After the first month, we brought in Michael Novelli to work with our volunteers, help model ways to improve using the story form, and answer any questions the leaders had. The biggest thing our leaders learned was how to look at the stories in new ways with each hearing and how to help students approach the stories in the same way.

As leaders and students have been able to move past the "I already know this story" mindset, they've discovered new and deeper insights from the stories. They're also seeing the story as a part of something bigger, realizing how one story flows into another and how they all become one interconnected narrative. I've found that as I get closer to the stories, I'm amazed at the details that are in them. But when I step back from the stories to see the whole story (or as much as I can see at this time), I'm amazed at the grandeur, depth, and beauty of God's Story.

One of our leaders, a great-grandmother and follower of Christ for longer than I've been alive, said, "I'm really enjoying using the stories; it's helping me to see God's Story in a new way once again." Another leader said, "It's caused me to go back and read God's Word to see if I really know the stories." Another leader said, "We've been using storying with our own kids for our family devotions because they enjoy listening to the stories and answering the questions."

Recently we finished the birth of Christ story. It was very powerful for us to see the Creator, who walked with Adam and Eve in the perfect garden, come again to walk with us in a broken world. The story challenged us to ask the question, *If we're following Jesus and imaging our Creator once again, then whom are we walking alongside in this broken world? To whom are we giving God's hope?* It also helped me to see Christmas through new eyes. This Christmas was very different for our family. Before we opened gifts on Christmas morning, we took gifts to a family that's been struggling financially. I believe we learned the importance of reaching out to this other family by really looking at the Christmas story in greater detail and as a part of God's larger ongoing story of redemption, hope, and love.

One of my students, a senior in high school, shared that she'd "heard these stories my entire life, [but] now I'm hearing them again in our small groups…and I'm still learning new things. I'm learning so much more in depth now."

I'm thankful for this resource and how it's helped me and my students view God's Story through new eyes.

—MATT DEJA, YOUTH WORKER IN GRAND RAPIDS, MICHIGAN

There are lots of books and resources on how to become a good storyteller. Here are two I've found helpful:

The Art of Storytelling: Easy Steps to Presenting an Unforgettable Story
John Walsh, Moody Press, 2003

The Storyteller's Start-Up Book: Finding, Learning, Performing and Using Folk-Tales
Margaret Read MacDonald, August House, 1993

5. HELP THE GROUP RETELL THE NEW STORY

It may seem redundant to retell a story you just told, but trust me—repetition is one of the most effective ways to learn. It builds retention and confidence, and it encourages your students to be more attentive to the story. Retelling should focus on recounting key events and dialogue from the story, not necessarily a word-for-word restating.

Spice it up. The key to retelling is variety. Try activities that will connect with different types of learners. Retelling exercises can be done in many ways (some creative ideas are provided in Appendix B).

Have fun and laugh together. This will help your group grow closer.

Learn from your listeners. Retelling will give you new insights into how well your group is listening and allow you to see the story from different viewpoints.

Keep it simple. Don't get bogged down in the details—celebrate what your students have learned.

RETELLING EXAMPLE

(If your group is large, then you may want to break it down into smaller groups—but have them all do the same exercise.)

You can say something like the following—

Now it's your job to act out the story! Here's how this will work...

1. Make a list of key events, dialogue, and characters. Don't add stuff or make stuff up. And no looking in the Bible—this exercise helps you dig into your memory.

2. Pick a storyteller and acting parts. And everyone has to be involved! That means someone might have to be a tree or an animal.

3. The actors will reenact the story as the narrator tells it. That means that as you tell your story, you'll need to stop at key points, such as, "Then Eve took a bite of the fruit." So you'd pause until "Eve" has acted out biting the fruit. Basically, the actors will be responding to, acting out, or repeating whatever the narrator says. Does that make sense?

4. Have fun and be creative! Use whatever props you can find or make.

I'm going to give the groups about 10 minutes to plan out their retelling, then we'll come back together and tell each scene. Go!

As soon as your groups finish planning their presentations (or after 10 minutes are up), have them retell the story.

If you have multiple groups, after one group finishes its retelling, ask the other students:

- What was your favorite part about their retelling?
- Were there any details that they should have included?

If you noticed something major that the group missed, ask questions to help the group remember it.

Details about the **Dialogue** and **Connecting** segments are in the next chapter.

QUESTIONS FOR RESPONSE AND DISCUSSION

Which parts of this chapter did you relate to your own story?

Who is the best storyteller you know? What makes that person a great storyteller?

What do you think is important in creating the right environment for storying?

What creative ways might you use to help your group review and retell Bible stories?

NOTES

1. Jay Cross, *Informal Learning: Rediscovering the Natural Pathways That Inspire Innovation and Performance* (San Francisco: Pfeiffer, 2006), 238.

LEADING AN EFFECTIVE DIALOGUE
CHAPTER 11

LEADING A STORYING DIALOGUE

Dialogue time is the solidifying piece in the storying process. Dialogue is where connections are made, key truths emerge, and the story becomes "our" story.

Dialogue time is the key to effective storying.

Questions are used to direct the participants to discover personal insights from the stories. In the narratives I've provided, questions lead participants to focus on wondering (feelings), remembering (facts), and connecting (implications).

In order to keep the group focused, a dialogue time always points to the story just told and its connection to the previous stories in the chronology.

STORYING DIALOGUE IS INTENTIONAL AND OPEN-ENDED

Open-ended in the sense that many questions have more than one correct response. *Open-ended* doesn't mean that the process is without guidance and direction. In fact, storying dialogue is *extremely intentional*. The dialogue questions in my narratives are carefully crafted and put in intentional order to help participants think deeply about the events and characters in each story—especially about the nature of God.

Because of storying's open-ended approach, some may fear it can become relativistic. On the contrary, storying dialogue isn't a loose discussion where any response is valid. The Bible stories provide the boundaries for interpretative missteps to be challenged. Participants are gently asked, "What did the story say about that?" and the group helps keep discussions on track through *communal correcting* (see the section in chapter 7, "Is Storying Biblically Accurate?" for more on communal correcting).

BECOME AN IMAGINATION CATALYST

The goal of the dialogue time is *listening, discovery, and connection.* Our role is to help participants fully engage in the process of learning. Through inspired dialogue we help students activate their imaginations and explore what God has for them in his Story.

That means we value what the story means for each individual, rather than focusing on what we feel is relevant. This is hard for us to do. We want others to come to the same understanding we have. The goal of storying is never to come to a consensus on what the story means. It's to come to God's Story as humble learners, with awe and wonder, embracing the mystery and complexity, expecting to encounter the Divine. Remember, God's Story is "alive and active" (Hebrews 4:12). Only the Holy Spirit can truly bring understanding and meaning to the things of God.

Sarah Arthur, in her book *The God-Hungry Imagination*, challenges us to "respect what the Holy Spirit is doing in the imaginations of your students. Don't try to manipulate, interpret, or explain the story away. You cannot forcibly open ears. Moreover, you may not be around when they begin to understand what the story is about...Allow a story to have multiple layers of meaning, more like an onion than a puzzle. And give your students the freedom and luxury to unpeel the onion at their own pace."[1]

SETTING EXPECTATIONS WITH YOUR GROUP

Dialogue time should have a different feel from the story and retelling segments. This is a time in which full participation is critical, and the energy must be high. You want to provide a healthy level of anticipation in your group, letting them know that you have high expectations and you value their input. (In larger groups, the person leading the dialogue can be different than the storyteller.)

Establish an environment of respect and value where students know they can't be critical of others. Any type of put-down will inhibit students from learning and speaking up. When students sense they're not in a safe place, you know as well as I do that they often disengage.

1. SHARE YOUR HOPES

Before you begin your first dialogue time, share your hopes for the group. Let them know that you believe God will speak through them, and they will learn from each other. Express your desire to be a colearner in the process. Emphasize that everyone is expected to participate, and that each person's observations matter—this is not about "right" answers; it's about "turning the diamond" (see chapter 7). Let them know that this process is different from anything they've experienced before. It's more rewarding, and it will require some effort and focus in order to learn.

2. SET SOME BOUNDARIES

Any good group discussion must have boundaries to ensure that everyone has a voice and your time remains on track. Before (or instead of) giving your list of boundaries, you may want to have your group work together to come up with their own list, asking them: "What do you think it would take for us to have a great dialogue time together?"

Here are some of the basics:

- No jumping ahead to future stories—only connecting to stories we've already covered in the chronology.

- Everyone's expected to share in the discussion—without being subjected to interruptions or put-downs.

- Many of the questions center on things you notice, connections you make, and questions you have.

- For many of the questions, there is no "right answer." That means questions and disagreements will come up, and that's okay. They're a part of the process.

- It's also okay for you (and me) to say, "I don't know."

- You may ask each other questions about the story—in fact, I encourage this!

You'll need to regularly revisit the list of boundaries with your students—especially during the first few weeks. Remember, repetition is good!

(Specific examples of how to set up your dialogue time are in Appendix B.)

PUTTING STORIES IN PERSPECTIVE

Some people struggle with the idea of interacting with the Bible as a story. They may be afraid that the stories will be overly paraphrased or that important details will be left out. Don't be defensive or draw unnecessary attention to these concerns, but briefly give proper perspective to how we're using these stories.

If you're using my narratives, then you may want to read the section in this book about how they were developed (pages 74-75) or make a brief comment about this. As you begin your discussion, you could say something like—

> I hope you were really engaged by that story. We wish we had enough time to go through every detail of it, but hopefully this experience will get you interested in learning more. You can find that story in the Bible. It's in the book of _____. Write down these verses so you can read more at home.
>
> In order to keep our discussion focused for now, we're going to talk about the details from the story we just heard. So if you have some insights you want to share from the Bible that are outside of this story, let's save that for the end of our time, okay?

TYPES OF DIALOGUE QUESTIONS

The narratives I've provided include dialogue questions that are designated as *wondering, remembering*, and *connecting* questions. These distinctions are intended to help the discussion leader and participants understand the desired kinds of responses.

1. WONDERING QUESTIONS (FEELINGS)

These questions help participants share what they're noticing about the story. Wondering questions are *divergent*, meaning that responses can go in a myriad of directions with many acceptable answers. Wondering questions bring energy to your group, inviting and inspiring new and creative insights. When asking wondering questions, you're not looking for specific or "right" answers but trying to spark imaginative responses.

Some sample wondering questions...

- "When you listened to this story, what did you see in your mind?"
- "How would you feel if you were in the boat with Jesus?"

- "What did you notice for the first time in this story?"
- "What does this story make you wonder about?"

IMPORTANT: *I **always** begin with at least one wondering question!* It's essential that you do this. Why? you may ask. Because wondering questions—

- Set a tone that you're not looking for "Sunday school" answers
- Give a sense of freedom that the students' observations and feelings matter
- Help the listeners think about the stories as real-life events
- Allow students to use their imaginations and creativity—areas unreached in most small groups
- Make it okay to wonder and have questions about the Bible
- Give students a sense of freedom to explore the stories instead of trying to dissect them

Wondering questions really helped disarm my students and allowed them to use their imaginations. When students asked questions about the story out of wonder (for instance, "Who was Cain afraid would attack him if he and his family were the first humans?"), I wouldn't give my opinion or an expert's answer. I'd just affirm them, saying, "That's a great question; I wonder about that, too," or "Would someone be willing to research that a bit this week and share what you learn the next time we meet?"

This took some getting used to for the students because they expected me, the Bible teacher, to give them all the answers. By allowing this kind of wondering and tension, we provided space for the stories to become real events in our minds. The stories became bigger than just allegories and fairy tales because we began looking at them from a different perspective.

2. REMEMBERING QUESTIONS (FACTS)

These questions help participants recount specific details from the story. Remembering questions are *convergent*, meaning that they draw participants toward particular responses and correct answers. These questions promote comprehension by encouraging participants to put what they remember into words. When asking remembering questions, you're looking for participants to accurately recount what happened in the story.

Some sample remembering questions...

- "What did God create in this story?"
- "What were the consequences of Adam and Eve's decision?"

If my group remembers most of the details of the story during the retelling, I'm apt to skip over some of the remembering questions.

3. CONNECTING QUESTIONS (IMPLICATIONS)

These questions stir participants to think about how the story connects to their own lives. I provide several of these questions for each story, but I generally choose one to center on for our connection time.

When asking connecting questions, allow ample time for your group to process and respond. I often give my group time to write down their responses and share them in smaller groups.

When responding to connecting questions, some students tend to be too general and some get "preachy," telling the rest of the group how they need to apply the story. Challenge participants to instead share *PERSONAL* applications and meaning. It also helps if you ask for responses to begin with, "The story challenged ME to..."

Some sample connecting questions...

- "What do you believe it means to be created in the image of God?"
- "How did this story challenge or encourage you?"

I recommend setting aside a separate time or group for connecting. (I'll provide more suggestions for your connection time later in this chapter.)

KEYS TO STORYING DIALOGUE

There's an art to leading a dialogue well—it's a careful balance of pacing, listening, connecting observations, and asking good follow-up questions. Storying dialogue is a process that's difficult to describe, and it takes practice to do it effectively. Here are some things that are important to keep in mind as you begin this journey:

ALLOW TIME FOR THINKING AND SHARING

Don't be afraid of silence. People need time to think about the question before expressing their thoughts out loud. By waiting after you ask a question, you cultivate an expectation that you really want students to thoughtfully respond.

I have to work hard at this. I get impatient when my group isn't answering right away, and I almost immediately begin to rephrase the question or call on someone. I need to slow down a bit and put myself in the place of the students. If you relate to my impatience, try this approach next time you lead a discussion:

> Begin by stating your question in a relaxed and confident manner. When you finish, start counting silently to yourself, "One thousand and one, one thousand and two," and so on until you get to "one thousand and ten." This isn't a long period of silence, though it will seem like an eternity. Scan the room slowly, remaining calm and relaxed, as you count. Most often you won't have to wait this long for the first response. If your group isn't used to open-ended discussions, expect to count all the way to 10 several times during the first few weeks of meeting.

> If no one has responded when you finish your count to 10, remain calm and rephrase the question in a shorter, clearer form. Send the nonverbal message, "I'm comfortable with waiting; I can wait here all day!" This will help prompt students to respond. Then begin your second count to 10. Classroom teachers using this technique almost always see students respond before they pass "five" on their second count.[2]

It's critical that you model patience during your first few storying dialogue sessions in order for your group to become accustomed to sharing openly when you ask questions.

BE PRESENT AND ATTENTIVE

A big part of storying is caring for people in the process. Give the group your undivided attention. We must believe that what our students share has meaning for our lives, too. God has much to teach us through those we lead—listen to them! It's easy for us as discussion leaders to get impatient and distracted. We begin thinking about the next question, or we get tired of hearing students share similar responses. Don't ignore or look past a student when she's sharing. BE PRESENT! For example, smile expectantly and nod as students speak. Maintain eye contact. Look relaxed and genuinely interested. Try to never interrupt a student's response. If we're not engaged in what they're sharing, then students will read our body language and begin to feel unheard and unimportant.

HELP PARTICIPANTS DRAW INSIGHTS FROM STORY EVENTS

After insights are given, ask, "Where did we see that in the story?" This will help them recall and articulate where they saw it, and it may spark them to remember other occurrences in the stories where something similar happened. This will also encourage participants to look to the story for insights, as well as discourage tangents.

EMBRACE PERPLEXITY AND MYSTERY

One of the great things about storying is that it sparks our imagination. We begin to envision the stories as reality. I love asking my group, "What do you wonder about from this story? What questions does it bring about?" This brings about all kinds of questions and curiosity. *How did the serpent move before it crawled on its belly?* This is good! Wondering about God and his Story helps us to realize that God is bigger and more creative than we thought. Participants will learn and think more for themselves if you leave room for unanswered questions, tension, mystery, and wonder. Think of your job as creating a safe environment for chaos and a crisis of faith.

ENCOURAGE CONNECTIONS TO PREVIOUS STORIES (NOT FUTURE ONES)

One of the most powerful parts of the storying experience is seeing people make connections between the stories. Encourage this by asking questions such as, "Where have you seen God do that before in the stories?" While looking backward is good, looking forward is a no-no! People may be eager to make connections to the life of Jesus while you're still in the Old Testament; gently encourage them to not jump ahead and really dig into the story at hand!

KEEP THE CONVERSATION GOING

Questions and curiosity drive learning. Once learners believe they have all the answers, they stop asking questions, and then they soon stop learning. Become an expert at redirecting questions back to the group...sparking further conversation and wondering. This will create an environment where deep learning can more readily take place. Don't be content with just one answer; ask what others in the group are thinking until several people have had the opportunity to answer.

Here are some ways you can keep the conversation going, adapted from Karen Lee-Thorp's *How to Ask Great Questions:*[3]

- Clarifying—Can you tell me a little bit more?
- Question—Where have we seen this happen before?
- Follow-Up—Why do you think that is?
- Bouncing—That's a great question. Does anyone in the group have any thoughts on that?
- Brainstorming—Let's see how many ideas our group can come up with...
- Sharing—I also noticed the connection between...
- Answering—In the story the character said...
- Bringing New Observations—One thing no one mentioned was...
- Identifying Themes—What did we see in this story that we also saw in previous ones?
- Summarizing—So what was one thing that stood out to you from the story?
- Prompting—Who would like to share what they journaled about?
- Restating—So what you're saying is...
- Connecting—What you're saying is connected to what Tom said...
- Feedback—How are you feeling about this process so far? What's helpful? What's challenging?
- Refocusing—That's a really interesting thought, but let's get back to the question I asked...
- Identifying—How do you think we're like the people in the story? Unlike them?
- Applying—How does this story challenge you personally?

INVOLVE QUIET STUDENTS

When I lead a dialogue, I try to make sure everyone is engaged and sharing observations. If someone isn't responding to the questions, I'll call on him. I've noticed that occasionally calling on people who aren't sharing helps build greater attentiveness in the group. But this must be done with tact and sensitivity.

We must keep in mind that quiet students aren't necessarily disengaged from the discussion. Sometimes those who are a bit more reserved are tracking with the discussion and intellectually active as participants. It's often the quiet students who share the most profound and deep observations. We must help allow space in the dialogue for them to feel safe to share their thoughts. If your group is active and engaged, a quiet student might not feel like her input is needed and won't interrupt to be heard.

Some things I've found to help engage quieter students:

- Asking them to share opinions and "wonderings"—something that doesn't call for a correct response. These types of questions are less threatening.

- Making it a point to give them a little extra encouragement when they share.

- Giving them outlets to share in smaller groups and through other mediums (art, music, poetry, etc.).

- Providing opportunities for them to write their responses before sharing them out loud.

- Sitting next to a quiet (or problematic) student. Proximity to the leader sometimes draws such students into dialogue.

REDIRECT TANGENTS

Crazy stuff might (and probably will) be said in your storying group. Tangents will fly like bottle rockets. You'll have to be sensitive enough to others—and to the Holy Spirit—to know when to rein it in. You'll have to be skilled enough to redirect and challenge learners to keep thinking, sharing, and digging for real meaning.

DON'T KILL THE DISCUSSION

Youth ministry expert Grahame Knox suggests five sure-fire ways to avoid an embarrassing silence:

1. Don't ask questions that can be answered with one word (e.g., *Do you agree that God loves you?*)

2. Don't ask loaded questions that suggest the answer (e.g., *Our bodies are God's temple, so should we smoke?*)

3. Don't ask intimidating questions (e.g., *If you really loved God, what you would do?*)

4. Don't ask embarrassing questions (e.g., *What's your most frequent temptation?*)

5. Don't try to make people guess the answers you want (e.g., *What are the three great truths from this passage?*)

I'll add one more:

6. Don't use "Why?" or "Why not?" in your follow-up questions (because they make people feel as though they're defending their answers).

[from *Creative Bible Study Methods for Youth Leaders*, an ebook by Grahame Knox, 2007, pp. 10-11]

DISCOURAGE DISTRACTING OR INAPPROPRIATE QUESTIONS

Sometimes a student will ask a question to sidetrack the class, get attention, or just embarrass you. If possible, redirect the group with a new question. If what's asked has created too much distraction, tactfully address what about the question is inappropriate and move on.

Steer away from students who monopolize the discussion. The best way to avoid monopolizers is to have students raise their hands—this gives you the option to distribute the responses across the whole group. You can also direct the question to other students by saying, "I'd love to know what Jenny thinks about this."

If the monopolizer is a serious problem, speak to him or her after group time. Tell the student that you value his or her participation and need help getting more students involved in the discussion.

ALLOW "COMMUNAL CORRECTING" TO TAKE PLACE

The group will help each other to ensure that key details of the stories are recounted accurately and not missed. When people are corrected by the group, they're less likely to withdraw from the discussion than they are when a leader corrects them. Correcting just becomes a refining part of the conversation.

ENCOURAGE, ENCOURAGE, ENCOURAGE!

Each time we meet I remind my group members that God speaks through the Bible story, and they need to share what God illuminates to them. Not only do I believe this, but it also helps create a healthy level of reverence for what each member shares. It inspires them to have faith and listen intently to the story. After students share I often acknowledge and genuinely encourage them, saying things like, "That is a great insight" or "Great answer! I've never heard that before" or "Thank you for sharing."

SHARE YOUR OBSERVATIONS

Many have asked me, "Is it okay for me to share my observations if I'm leading the group?" My answer is always, "Yes! But never share first." The hardest part of leading others through Storying Dialogue is being patient and allowing the process to unfold. Don't try to be the expert—if the group knows you're going to give "the answers," they'll stop sharing.

Pick your spots to share appropriately so they don't squelch the learning process. In groups that I lead, I primarily share only my wonderings and questions from the stories. This shows the group that I'm also in awe of God and his stories.

Another question I'm asked is, *Should I answer when a student asks me a question about the Bible?*

Whenever possible, I try *not* to answer students' questions directly because it works against efforts to create a participative learning environment.

If I believe someone in the group can answer the question, I redirect it to the group. This not only encourages more student participation, but it also implies that peers are a resource for learning.

If I don't know the answer, I tell the group I don't know. If I think that the answer would be helpful and connect to what we are learning, I'll sometimes assign a student to research it before the next meeting.

If the question is a major tangent but still a good question, I'll try to postpone the answer, saying, "That's a really good question; why don't we talk about that at the end if we have time?" Then I also have the option to just give my response to a few students.

On rare occasions if a student asks me for my opinion about a Bible question, and I think it will help the group, I'll share my thoughts. Then I'll try to follow up my thoughts with a question (e.g., "If that's true about Abraham, what do you think that tells us about his relationship with God?")

Doug Pagitt, in his book *Preaching Re-Imagined*, encourages leaders to use provisional statements. In other words, "It seems to me…" "As I understand it…" and so on, in order to create "a culture of openness and invitation. These words make room for the thoughts and experiences of others."[4]

When I've felt the need to share a deeper thought about the story, I try to use provisional statements in the hope that they won't steamroll others and come across as the "right answers."

DIALOGUING ESSENTIALS

The goal of a storying dialogue is to encourage participants to share their observations and "wonderings" about the story.

Leading a dialogue requires us to…

- Let go…of the role of expert teacher and embrace the role of co-learner, encourager, and guide.

- Listen…in expectation that God is revealing himself to and through each person present.

- Trust…that God will work through the process, valuing the experience as much as the knowledge and content.

- Be patient...allowing time to process, room for different opinions, tangents, tension, questions, and wondering.

- Have faith...that God will speak and help bring to light the truth and implications he wants to reveal.

Storying dialogue requires a lot of patience, shepherding, encouragement, and practice. After a few stories, participants will get into the rhythm of this process, and they will begin to really listen and think deeply about the story.

LEADING A CONNECT TIME

In my youth group, we had a separate time for connecting the story. After our dialogue time, we broke up into gender-specific small groups. We sometimes called these "my story" groups, as the focus was sharing ways we saw our stories connecting with God's and with each other's. We focused these times on prayer, caring for each other, and sharing how we saw God shaping us. Toward the beginning of the year, we took turns sharing our personal stories in these groups.

We never told the students how to apply the stories, but we did ask some pointed questions, such as, "How does this story challenge or encourage you to live?" These times were filled with honesty and amazing insights from our students.

Each week I distributed cards with the Scriptures listed for that week's story. Without my prompting, students were coming back the next week with observations and questions after reading more about the story! The story began sparking a desire to learn more and actually read the Bible. A few of the students told me they studied the stories as part of their devotional time each day.

One of the ways we helped further encourage students' connection with the story at our Merge event was through *Response Stations*. Each day, students were guided toward expressing a response at their choice of three stations: Art Expression (HEART), Study and Discussion (MIND), or Prayer and Reflection (SOUL). The focus of these stations was to provide an opportunity for students to share how they were seeing their story connect with God's. These stations were followed by a time of sharing what we were learning from the stories. Students shared through art, poetry, and testimony how the story was affecting their lives. It was incredibly meaningful.

Storying connection time is neccesary to help students apply what they're learning to real life. Plan time and activities that help students process how they're seeing God's Story connect to their stories.

QUESTIONS FOR RESPONSE AND DISCUSSION

Which parts of this chapter did you relate to your own story?

Who is the best discussion leader you know? What makes this person so great?

What are some of the challenges with leading a storying dialogue?

How is this different than some of the discussion or small-group leader roles you've experienced?

What are some ways you can spark your group's imagination and creativity?

What do you believe it takes to be an effective storying dialogue leader?

NOTES

1. Sarah Arthur, *The God-Hungry Imagination: The Art of Storytelling for Postmodern Youth Ministry* (Nashville, Tenn: Upper Room Books, 2007), 149.
2. Adapted from the online article from the University of Oklahoma, "Ideas on Teaching: Leading Discussions" and based on materials from *Mastering the Techniques of Teaching,* Joseph Lowman (2nd ed., Jossey-Bass, San Francisco, 1995, http://www.ou.edu/pii/tips/ideas/discussions.html)
3. Karen Lee-Thorp, *How to Ask Great Questions: Guide Your Group to Discovery With These Proven Techniques* (Colorado Springs, Col.: NavPress, 1998).
4. Doug Pagitt, *Preaching Re-Imagined: The Role of the Sermon in Communities of Faith* (Grand Rapids, Mich.: Zondervan, 2005), 40.

BEGINNING YOUR STORYING ADVENTURE...
CONCLUSION

The Bible is alive, it speaks to me; it has feet, it runs after me; it has hands, it lays hold of me.

—MARTIN LUTHER

Storying has changed my life. It has helped me and many others to listen to the Scriptures in a new way. I regularly get emails from small group leaders, youth workers, and students who've been transformed by God through Bible storying. Their stories are faith inspiring and humbling. Here are a couple of responses that have stuck with me...

"My students were immersed in the Scriptures in a way they have never been before. They have a greater understanding of the Story of Stories. They became a part of the Story! This was an opportunity for us to engage in a life-changing experience."

—DAVID, YOUTH WORKER

"The stories came alive to our students—the more they talked about them, the more they saw different ways they connected to their lives. They were learning for themselves—and this learning sticks! I was right there with the students...the stories came alive for me, too!" —RACHEL, VOLUNTEER

"I began to see the context of my life within God's story. The Bible's not distant any-more. It's like—whoa!—my life has merged with God's Story. I'm part of what God is doing. I'm a kingdom participant and builder. I realize that community is the most important thing I could give my life to. That's what its all about—a bunch of people getting together to live collectively and individually the life Jesus came to show us."
—NATALIE, HIGH SCHOOL SENIOR

God's Story can shape our lives in profound ways. When we allow ourselves to be captured by this amazing story, it reveals to us how we were created to live and what role we play in bringing God's love and restoration to the world.

To be shaped by God's Story requires "a willingness to take a step of faith—to enter the simplicity of the stories to discover the complexity that lies beyond...giving our selves to the story in hope and belief that God will meet us there. It is as Jesus said, 'Unless you become like a child, you shall not enter the kingdom of God.' It is standing under to understand...like a child...and to be swept away by God's Story." (H. Stephen Shoemaker, *GodStories: New Narratives from Sacred Texts*, Judson Press, Valley Forge, PA, 1998, xxv)

We're on this adventure together...a journey into the divine mystery and beauty of God. Storying acts as a map to guide us toward discovering the amazing power of God's Story. This adventure is not easy...storying is unpredictable, unsettling, full of wonder and moments of awakening. But we must move into uncharted waters, embarking on a new path of learning that asks a lot from our students and us. The reward of this adventure is great...a community of people transformed by God, ready to change the world.

Together, may we truly be shaped by the story.

RESOURCES
SHAPED BY THE STORY

APPENDIX A:
USING THE *SHAPED BY THE STORY* DVD

If you haven't discovered it, there is a companion DVD in the back of this book. Bonus! Here are some details about this special resource:

WHY DID I INCLUDE A DVD?

Bible Storying is something that is best experienced rather than just explained. It is a unique process that has specific rhythms and nuances to it. My hope is that the book and DVD will work in tandem, like a mini-workshop for your leaders.

WHAT IS ON THE DVD?

Storying Promo Video

This three-and-a-half minute video was designed to help YOU communicate with **parents**, **church leaders**, and **students** about the benefits of Bible storying. The excitement and experiences of the students and leaders in this video will help spark interest and enthusiasm as you begin storying with your group.

Story and Dialogue Process

This section of the DVD takes you inside a real youth group as they experience the story of Adam and Eve's separation. The responses are completely genuine and unscripted. Before each segment I offer leader's tips and things to look for.

Extended Interviews

In these interviews students and youth workers describe their experiences with Bible storying.

Discussion Questions

If you are using this DVD as a training tool, you can select this special track to help facilitate a discussion with your leaders.

I am so excited that you are beginning your adventure in Bible Storying. If you need further encouragement, training, ideas, or have questions, please visit www.echothestory.com.

I hope and pray that you and your group will truly be Shaped by God's Story!

APPENDIX B:
INTERACTIVE IDEAS FOR STORYING

The ideas in this appendix are divided into segments corresponding to the storying process:

1. Sharing the IMPORTANCE OF STORY (Pre-Storying)
2. Preparing Your Group for IMAGINATIVE LISTENING
3. Engaging Participants during STORYTELLING / NARRATING
4. REVIEWING and RETELLING the Story as a Group
5. CONNECTING the Story to Your Own Lives

Their are two different kinds of ideas: Interactive exercises and "set-ups." Set-ups are scripts that help you to explain different aspects of storying to your group.

This is an ever-growing list of ideas—to see the most current list or contribute your own ideas, go to www.echothestory.com.

SHARING THE IMPORTANCE OF STORY

I've found it helpful to spend time with my group considering the importance of stories BEFORE engaging in storying. This helps groups to begin to see how stories shape us, and how they can look at the Bible as a story. Here are some ideas that can be used together or separately:

IDEA 1: CHILDHOOD STORIES

Have participants share about one of their favorite stories from their childhood. It could be a family story that was passed down or a story from a book. Ask, "Who told you this story? What did you like about it?"

IDEA 2: HAVE PARTICIPANTS BRING EXAMPLES OF THEIR FAVORITE STORIES FROM A BOOK OR A MOVIE. HAVE THEM SHARE...

OPTION A: SHARING OUR FAVORITE STORY

- a favorite "scene" from the story in 30 seconds or less (i.e. reading an excerpt, or showing a movie clip)

- a summary of the story, including the setting and main characters

- how they have identified with a character(s) in the story

- how the characters may have changed in the story

- why they love the story and what makes it a good story

- how the story has affected their life

OPTION B: FINDING THE PARTS OF A STORY

- main characters – The characters who are involved in the important actions in the story

- supporting characters – Minor characters who help us learn about the main characters

- character development – The way a character learns and grows as a result of her experiences in the story

- setting – The time and place of a story

- plot – The sequence of events

- problem – The conflict in a story that the main character or characters must face

- resolution – How the problem in the story is resolved or left at the end

OPTION C: STORY MAPPING

See page 111. Additional idea: Research and share how all good stories are based on THE GREAT STORY. See the book *Reel Spirituality: Theology and Film in Dialogue* by Robert Johnston, Baker Books, 2000.

IDEA 3: CONNECTING WITH STORIES

Share and discuss a quotation or excerpt from chapter 6, "Connecting with Story." I recommend using the quotation from Mark Miller on how "stories are viewed from the lens of the soul."

IDEA 4: STORIES THAT SHAPE US

Ask participants to write or share about a personal story that has shaped them, providing a few instructions: Write out the details of the story as best as you can remember it. Tell it as a story on paper. Then, describe how that story has changed the way you think, act and live.

IDEA 5: THE GREAT STORY

Have participants answer the question, "What is the Bible's story?"Have participants dewscribe the essence of the Bible story in their own words in one page or less. Then discuss misconceptions (yours and theirs):

- How do we often start the story in the middle or towards the end with Jesus?

(Show a movie in the middle and ask students to tell you beginning and end. My friend Seth showed a short segment from the middle of one of the Lord of the Rings movies. Then he asked his students to describe the events that led up to that scene. Seth made the point that we need to know the entire story—from the beginning—in order to really understand each scene.)

- Why do we often think of the Bible as a bunch of disconnected stories?
- Why do we sometimes think of the Bible as a story that doesn't apply to today?

IDEA 6: GOD'S BIG PICTURE

Read together the book, *God's Big Picture: Tracing the Storyline of the Bible* by Vaughn Roberts, IVP, 2002. It is a great overview of the Bible Story, easy enough to read for high school students.

IDEA 7: THE BIG STORY

Read together the book, *The Big Story: What Actually Happens in the Bible* by Nick Page, Authentic Publishing, 2007. It's a fun, easy-to-read version of the key narratives in the Bible.

PREPARING YOUR GROUP FOR IMAGINATIVE LISTENING

You'll need to be intentional in helping your group refocus by coaching them to be attentive listeners. Here are some ideas to help you set up your storytelling time:

REMEMBER: Your storytelling time needs to take a different tone from the rest of your group time—a slower, more focused pace. You'll need to set the tone for this, letting students know that it's a special time and they'll need to work hard at concentrating and getting into "storying mode." To help them get started, you may want to light a candle to signify storying as a holy practice.

IDEA 1: IMAGINATIVE LISTENING EXERCISE

- Ask participants to define what they think imaginative listening is and what it takes to be a good imaginative listener.

- Tell a story or use an audio book segment—2-4 minutes max—not from the Bible

- Have students use imaginative listening to "enter" and remember the story...

- They can draw, write, close their eyes, find a focal point, etc.

- Ask students to share what they saw, felt, smelled, heard in their minds as they listened to the story.

IDEA 2: TURNING THE DIAMOND

"Right now, we're going to try a new approach to learning from the Bible called "storying." This unique approach is rooted in the ancient Hebrew way of learning through careful observation and dialogue."

Shine a light through a magnifying glass and ask, "What does this magnifying glass do to the light?" After some responses from the students, say, "Right... it intensifies it and focuses it. We often come to the Bible like this—which is not necessarily bad—but we are intensely looking at one verse or section for a single answer. We are narrowing our focus."

Shine the light through a prism and ask, "What does this prism do to the light? How is this different than the magnifying glass?" After some responses from the students say, "A prism is kind of like a diamond in that it has many sides, that reflect light all around."

"The Hebrew people had a unique way of looking at the Scriptures... they called it the Seventy Faces of Torah—the Torah being the first five books of the Bible. They got this phrase by comparing the Scriptures to a beautiful diamond with 70 sides—or faces (like a prism).

Hearing and studying the Scriptures was likened to holding up and turning that diamond—allowing the light to reflect further beauty, depth, detail, and brilliance.

Just like the ancient Hebrews, we believe that the Bible and its stories are living, and have meaning and mystery that we can discover today. We must choose now to turn the diamond, looking for more that's within in the story. We do this expecting God to illuminate something new to each one of us.

When you see something in the story—something simple, or beautiful or profound—you need to share it with the group! That's how we learn through storying—we listen to all of the different reflections from God's story. Each one is important and can teach us something new.

This process isn't easy—it takes concentration and something called "imaginative listening." What do you think it means to be an imaginative listener?

(*Imaginative listening* means using your imagination to picture the story in your mind like you would a movie, where you are actually in the scene.)

After we're done listening to this story, we'll retell it as a group. Pay attention to the details of the story because I will ask you about them! If it helps you to concentrate, you may close your eyes during the story, write down your thoughts, or choose a focal point to look at in the room.

Are you ready? Take a moment in silence to slow down and clear your mind.

Whisper a prayer asking God to speak to you through his story.

IDEA 3: IMPLICATION VS. APPLICATION

(This idea is best used after you have gone through several of the stories already with your group.) Ask, "What do you think some of our goals in reading the Bible should be?" (Get responses from the group.)

"Often times our goal in reading the Bible is to find a specific application—something useful for our life. That is a good thing to desire...to find application means to put something on, or to apply it to a specific situation and find it useful. When we discover application for our lives, it tends to be more of an external help, like putting a Band-Aid or balm on a cut. (Take out some Band-Aids and hand them out as a visual.) The problem with application is that it often focuses more on our outward actions and not enough on our internal condition.

It feels more like a quick fix to a problem—it does not change our motivations on the inside and answer the question, "Why should I love differently?"

"The beauty of stories is that they do more than give us application points...they implicate us. What do you think that means—to be implicated?" (get some responses from the group).

"We become wrapped up in stories...to implicate means to connect, tie, or knit together (use a rope as a visual). Stories implicate us like strands of a rope wound together...stories become a part of who we are and change our motivations. They do more than give us external answers—they shape our internal lives and values."

Ask, "How have you identified with the Bible stories we've told? How might they be shaping your life?"

IDEA 4: YOU ARE NOW THE TEACHERS

"If you are really listening and entering the story, I believe that God's Spirit will illuminate things to you from the story. That means they will stand out in your mind and you will connect with them in a new way. It may be something unique or simple or beautiful or profound about God. It may be a connection between the stories you realized for the first time. When this happens (and it will), you need to share it with the group. We need each of you to share what you're seeing in the story...because you are now the teachers helping the rest of the group learn and discover the depth of the story."

IDEA 5: EXPECTANCY

"I am expecting everyone to share and participate today! Each of one your observations and perspectives is important and needed in this process. I will call on you if I need to, but I'd prefer if you would just share your thoughts without being prompted. Are you ready?"

IDEA 6: GET SOME FEEDBACK

"Are you getting into the rhythm of this discussion time? What is different about storying than other discussion groups you have been a part of? What do you like about it? What is challenging about it?"

IDEA 7: NO LONGER CHILDREN

"You don't come to these stories as children anymore...or even as you did just a year ago. You're growing into adults, and God is expanding your mind and desiring to show you new things. These stories aren't the entire picture of God's plan. It's kind of like we're gazing out of a skylight—we see just a glimpse of the expansive sky overhead. This story is just a glimpse of how big and how awesome God is. As God shows you new things, he desires for you to share them with us so we can see more of who God is with you."

ENGAGING PARTICIPANTS DURING STORYTELLING

Storytelling is more like the work of an artist than that of a teacher. It's less about explaining and more about exploring. Our role is to help each other participate in the stories of God. As we participate in these stories, they become our own—the gospel happens to us.

For some more details about how to be an effective storyteller, please see chapter 10.

IDEA 1: SLOWING DOWN

Before I tell each story, I say something like this: "After we're done listening to this story, we'll retell it as a group. Pay attention to the details of the story because I will ask you about them! If it helps you to concentrate, you may close your eyes during the story, write down your thoughts, or choose a focal point to look at in the room.

Are you ready? Take a moment in silence to slow down and clear your mind. Whisper a prayer asking God to speak to you through his story."

IDEA 2: JOURNAL PAGES

For many people, including me, writing or drawing while we listen can help us to concentrate. To connect with people who are this way, I have provided "journal pages" for them to use during the storytelling. These pages would contain a lot of space for them to write or draw, and Scripture references for the story to study later. Immediately following the story I would provide time for the entire group to journal their responses. I've found that this helps many of the students better articulate their observations during the dialogue time.

Here are some of the Journal Questions to answer for every story:

Listen... draw... write... Capture key details from this story that stand out to you here:

(leave lots of space after this...at least a half-page)

What did you see, hear, and feel when you were listening to this story?

What did you notice in this story for the first time?

What do you wonder about? What questions did it bring up?

Which of the characters in this story are you sometimes like? How?

Based on this story what do you think God desires from people? From you?

REVIEWING AND RETELLING THE STORY AS A GROUP

Try to spend 25 minutes or less on your Retelling, and 10 minutes or less on Review. Make sure your Review and Retelling times are fun and full of energy—that starts with you! Carefully choose volunteers and gravitate toward group members who will engage others with their enthusiasm. You are the best gauge if something is engaging with your group—if something is not working, MOVE ON to the next activity!

IDEA 1: WHOLE GROUP RETELLING

After telling each story (or scene), invite the group to participate in the retelling by saying, "In order to help us really enter this story, we are going to retell the events in the order they happened while it is still fresh in your mind. You will be surprised at how much you remember! For the next story, I would love to see one of you retell the story by yourself. So, be listening carefully to the details. What happened first in this story?"

Ask follow-up questions that guide the group (i.e., "What did God say to them after that?" and, "What was Moses' reaction?"). This does not need to be an exact retelling; it should be a quick overview catching key events and dialogue in order.

If someone jumps way ahead in the story, affirm them and say, "Right—that did happen. Hold that thought, and I will come right back to you. Can someone tell me what happened before that?"

If the group misses something, you may want to fill it in. But push the group through follow-up questions and hints to let THEM remember and retell the story. retelling may seem a bit redundant, but it is an excellent exercise to help them think deeply about the story.

IDEA 2: INDIVIDUAL RETELLING

Ask the group if someone would like to try and retell the entire story. Let them know they can have a friend help them. The rest of the group (and the leader) will not interrupt or help, unless the person retelling asks for it. Make sure you have the group cheer them on after the retelling! If they missed some details, gently ask the group "Is there anything else from that story that you remember that they didn't mention?"

IDEA 3: TAG-TEAM RETELLING

Group members tell a portion of the story (at least one sentence), then tag another group member to continue where they left off. If they missed some details, ask the group, "Is there anything else from that story that you remember that they didn't mention?"

Add "Then Suddenly…" The same as tag-team retelling, except each person has to end their part of the retelling with the phrase "Then suddenly.." This adds a fun twist to the retelling!

IDEA 4: KEY-EVENT SHUFFLE

Write out all of the key events in the story on pieces of paper—or find images for each event from the story. Mix up the order of these papers and give one to each person. Have the group try to put the events in order, and then have each person share details from their portion of the story.

IDEA 5: BIBLE STORYBOARDS

Ask participants to get into pairs, and provide them with a long strip of paper. Ask them to draw a series of pictures that retell the story and include captions where possible. Participants can then share their retelling with the rest of the group. Mention how different people see the story from different perspectives and emphasize different things they are seeing from the story.

IDEA 6: READ AROUND

Ask for volunteers to read a few lines of the narrative each as the rest of the group listens—like a "reader's theater."

IDEA 7: SILENT READ

Give out a copy of the narrative AFTER it has been told and have participants read it silently. This seems to work well if only done once in a while—if you do this every week your group may tend to get bogged down in the details of the words of the story.

IDEA 8: CHARACTER IDENTIFICATION

Hand out slips of paper with different characters or people groups that were present in the story. (It works even better if you can find images that represent each of the people groups). As you retell the story, ask them to identify with the character or people group they were given. After the retelling, ask, "What do you think your character was feeling in this story?" then ask, "How did listening from the perspective of your character change your perspective of this story?"

IDEA 9: CHOOSE AN EXPRESSION

Ask participants to get into groups of three. Have them choose from different creative expressions for their retelling: drawing, drama, writing (in their own words), spoken word, or music. Give each group two minutes to present their retelling to the rest of the group.

IDEA 10: ILLUSTRATE THE STORY

Ask your group to illustrate the story in pictures using paints, crayons, or pencils. Alternatively, create a collage using scrap materials (magazines, newspapers, scrap fabric or wool, cardboard boxes, etc.) or make a banner or mural using fabric or wallpaper.

IDEA 11: ACT IT OUT

Have volunteers "act out" different characters as the story is narrated aloud. The actors do not need to say anything, but just react as events happen in the story. The narrator should give cues, stopping after key events or dialogue to allow the actors to respond. Have fun with this!

IDEA 12: MODERN-DAY REMIX

Break into groups of two. Spend time having the groups come up with a modern-day version of the story. Ask each group to write out their own translation of the passage—as if they were emailing or telling this story to a friend. Most groups will do better if they spend time writing down their thoughts first, then reading them to the group!

IDEA 13: STORY COMMERCIAL

Have participants get into pairs and come up with a retelling of the story that is 30 seconds or less...like a commercial that grabs your attention!

IDEA 14: NEWS REPORT

Have your group put together a live news report that would retell the story, including eyewitness interviews! If you want to be more ambitious, use a camcorder to shoot a news bulletin, complete with newscaster, 'on-the-ground' reports, expert opinion, perhaps even a weather forecast!

IDEA 15: NEWSPAPER HEADLINE

Break into pairs and have each group come up with a newspaper headline and the first sentence of a news article about the story.

IDEA 16: CHARADES

Have volunteers from your group act out the story without using any words!

IDEA 17: SMALL GROUP RETELLING

Break into small groups and retell the story with each other. Have groups think about these questions:

Who were all of the characters in the story?

What were the major events in the story?

What can we learn from this story about God?

What can we learn about ourselves?

Bring the whole group back together, having each smaller group share their responses to the questions.

IDEA 18: PASS THE STORY

Pass a ball or object around the group. The person with the ball has to share what happened next in the story. Come up with your own rules for this! Some groups use a ball of yarn, un-raveling it as it's passed to show how the story and the group are interconnected.

IDEA 19: GROUP MURAL

Have your group create a "mural" on a large piece of paper that retells the story. Get everyone involved! Start by making a list of the major events in the story. If neccesary, assign parts of the story to different groups.

IDEA 20: SYMBOLS

I've used symbols during the review time, asking participants to draw them or identify the story that goes with each of them. My symbols are intentionally simple so anyone can draw and remember them (see below). You may even want to see if your group can come up with their own symbols. Have fun with this and be creative!

Say, "Can anyone tell me—in 30 seconds or less—what happened in our last story?" Get one or two students to give you a quick overview. Draw the symbols for the stories you've already covered. You may want to ask a student volunteer to draw these symbols each time.

IDEA 21: LECTIO DIVINA

Find a passage in the Bible that is central to the story you just told. I would provide this printed out for the participants or bookmarked in a Bible. Then, create a handout with all of the instructions below:

> *Lectio Divina* is Latin for "divine reading." This ancient practice helps us slow down, listen, and pray, looking for God to reveal himself to us through his Word.
>
> You will begin this exercise now, and then gather back together in your group in about 5 or 6 minutes. The goal of this time is to release all expectations, and to become more aware of God's presence. Before you begin reading, take a moment to clear your mind right now.

Take some deep breaths and pray, inviting the Holy Spirit to speak to you and help you focus during your prayer time.

Allow these steps to guide your time...

1. LECTIO—Read the passage on the next page slowly several times.

2. MEDITATIO – Reflect: What word or phrase stands out to you? What from this passage seems to speak to you directly?

3. ORATIO—Open your palms as you pray. Let God know that your heart, mind and soul are open to hearing from him now.

4. CONTEMPLATIO—Listen for God to speak or guide you in some way. Don't rush this listening time...if your mind wanders away from listening, refocus by praying and asking God to help you sense his nearness.

Repeat this process or go back to a part of it that was meaningful to you and connect with God. After about 5 or 6 minutes you will re-gather as a group and share how this time was meaningful to you.

Begin step 1 now by reading the passage from the story provided for you.

When you regather as a group, share…

How was this time meaningful for you?

What words or phrases stood out to you the most?

How does the passage from the story motivate you to live differently?

IDEA 22: REVIEW NIGHTS

Instead of doing a new story every week, plan some nights that focus just on looking back. Take regular opportunities (quarterly?) to review all of the stories you have told to that point using symbols and creative ideas.

SETTING UP THE STORY DIALOGUE

Dialogue time should have a different feel from the story and retelling segments. This is a time in which full participation is critical, and the energy must be high. You want to provide a healthy level of anticipation in your group, letting them know that you have high expectations and you value their input. Here are some specific things you can say to help prepare your group for a great dialogue time:

IDEA 1: BRAINSTORM GUIDELINES

Ask your group, "What do you think it would take for us to have a great dialogue time together?

"What could sidetrack us from a great dialogue?" Make a list of what the participants come up with.

IDEA 2: DIALOGUE BASICS

Here are some of the basics:

- No jumping ahead to future stories—only connecting to stories we've already covered in the chronology.

- Everyone gets a chance to share without interruption or put-downs.

- Many of the questions center around things you notice, connections you make, and questions you have.

- For many of the questions, there's not one "right answer." That means questions and disagreements will come up, and that's okay. They're a part of the process.

- It's also okay for you (and me) to say, "I don't know."

- You may ask each other questions about the story—in fact, I encourage this!

IDEA 3: DIALOGUE QUESTIONS

"Now we are going to talk about this story together. This discussion time might be different than Bible studies you've been a part of before...

1. Many of the questions I will ask are called WONDERING QUESTIONS such as, "What did you see in your mind when you were listening to the story?" These questions are to engage your imagination—to help you put yourself back in the scene.

2. I will also be asking REMEMBERING QUESTIONS, like, "What did God create in this story?"

Some of these questions will seem simple at first...but stop and think about them...dig in and find new meaning and connections in the stories.

3. The last kind of question I will ask is a CONNECTING QUESTION, like, "What do you think it means to be created in the image of God?" These questions help us to think and pray about how the story connects with our own lives.

4. Now, one important guideline...we're only going to talk about details from this story and any of the ones we've told before it. We're not going to jump ahead to Jesus, or share stuff that we already know. That may seem a little weird, but trust me, if we listen to these stories like it's the first time we've heard them, we will be able to go deeper. This also allows us all to be equals in this discussion.

Remember—these stories are like diamonds, you may see things reflected in this story that no one else sees. Share it! Each of us, in a real sense, becomes the teacher by sharing what God is showing us—we are here to learn from each other! Does this make sense? Any questions before we get started?"

IDEA 4: DON'T THROW AWAY YOUR BIBLE!

Some people struggle with the idea of interacting with the Bible as a story. They may be afraid that the stories will be overly paraphrased or that important details will be left out. Don't be defensive or draw unnecessary attention to these concerns, but briefly give proper perspective to how we're using these stories.

As you begin your discussion, you could say something like, "I hope you were really engaged by that story. We wish we had enough time to go through every detail of it, but hopefully this experience will get you interested in learning more. You can find that story in the Bible. It's in the book of _____. Write down these verses so you can read more at home.

In order to keep our discussion focused for now, we're going to talk about the details from the story we just heard. So if you have some insights you want to share from the Bible that are outside of this story, let's save that for the end of our time, okay?

"Be patient with this, we're going to try something new. We're not getting rid of our Bibles. In fact, I think this will get you more interested in reading them. You'll soon see how this matters in your life."

If you're using my narratives, then you may want to read the section in this book about how they were developed or make a brief comment about this.

CONNECTING THE STORY TO YOUR OWN LIVES

Storying connection time is necessary to help students apply what they're learning to real life. Plan time and activities that help students process how they're seeing God's Story connect to their stories.

IDEA 1: CONNECTING QUESTION

In my narratives I provide some "connecting" questions for each story. Select one or two of these questions ahead of time and have participants journal their response. EXAMPLE:

"Take a moment to think about this question. You can write out or draw a picture of your response." Then, regather as a whole group or in smaller groups and share your responses.

IDEA 2: CONNECTION GROUPS

Have participants get in groups of three and share their responses to the connection questions you select. If time permits, ask a few students to share their responses with the entire group.

In my youth group we focused these times on prayer, caring for each other, and sharing how we saw God shaping us. Toward the beginning of the year, we took turns sharing our personal stories in these smaller groups. Sometimes we even called these "My Story" groups to emphasize the connection between God's Story and ours.

IDEA 3: SCRIPTURE CARDS

Distribute cards with the Scriptures listed for that story and encourage students to expore the further story before you gather again. EXAMPLE: "FOR FURTHER EXPLORATION: This week read Genesis 1-2, Psalm 8, and Psalm 104. Next time we gather we'll share our new observations together!"

IDEA 4: RESPONSE STATIONS

One of the ways we helped further encourage students' connection with the story at our Merge event was through Response Stations. Each day, students were guided toward expressing a response at their choice of one of three stations: Art Expression (HEART), Study and Discussion (MIND), or Prayer and Reflection (SOUL). The focus of these stations was to provide an opportunity for students to share how they were seeing their story connect with God's. These stations were followed by a time of sharing what we were learning from the stories. Students shared through art, poetry, and testimony how the story was affecting their lives. It was incredibly meaningful.

These ideas could be done before or after the storying process...

IDEA 5: DISCOVERING MY OWN STORY

Develop a lesson / exercise on understanding your own story. Here are some good references: *To Be Told: God Invites You to Co-Author Your Future* by Dan Allender, WaterBrook Press, 2006. *Tell Me a Story: The Life-Shaping Power of Our Stories* by Daniel Taylor, Bog Walk Press, 2001 (good section in appendix about defining our stories).

IDEA 6: MY STORY PRESENTATION

Participants will narrate their own stories verbally, enhanced by creative means—video, pictures, collage, objects, song, stories, etc. Their presentations will seek to share their life as one continuous story, connecting important milestones and snapshots of their life.

IDEA 7: MY LIFE STORYBOARD

Participants will share their story by developing a "storyboard." As our story intersects with God's, we have a powerful and interesting story to tell. A good way to share our story is to look at it in snapshot form. Each participant should take a large piece of paper, and draw lines to divide it into nine equal boxes. Then, draw a picture for each of these nine areas:

1. One of my earliest memories as a child...

2. What my life was like growing up...

3. A significant event that has shaped my life...

4. A significant person who has shaped my life...

5. An important decision I made in my faith journey...

6. The most important people in my life and why...

7. How I am a part of God's story...

8. Areas God is changing in me now...

9. What I hope to see in my future...

Don't worry about artistic ability or about making the pictures too detailed. These will not be entered into an art competition—we promise! Write a word, phrase or sentence under each snapshot to help explain what you have drawn. Be Creative!! Have Fun!! Take ten to fifteen minutes to create your storyboard then share it, explaining each snapshot.

IDEA 8: HANDS-ON EXPERIENCES

I have been developing some experiential learning activities that help participants "enter" the story in deeper ways. These are walkthrough activities, such as a Tabernacle for participants to learn about by entering, and a Passover Seder. Hands-on activities take careful planning and extra creativity but they are worth it! I would love to hear your ideas, too—find out more about these activities at www.echothestory.com or www.mergeevent.com.

FURTHER CONNECTIONS TO THE STORY...

We are just beginning to explore ways to encourage participants to connect the story to their own lives. I will continually be adding ideas to **www.echothestory.com.**

APPENDIX C:
SAMPLE BIBLE NARRATIVE

STORY: CREATION

Story based on: Genesis 1-2, Psalm 8, Psalm 104, Psalm 103:19-22, Psalm 148:2-5, Isaiah 45:18, Nehemiah 9:5-7, Job 38:4-7

1. PREPARE FOR IMAGINATIVE LISTENING

For specific ideas to prepare your group for *Imaginative Listening* see Appendix B in this book or go to the ideas section on www.echothestory.com. (I recommend using the "Turning the Diamond" idea for this story.)

2. NARRATE THE STORY

This story, found in the ancient Scriptures, has been passed down for many generations. And it begins like this:

Before anything existed was The Creator....a great and mysterious being called God.

As God began forming the earth, angels watched in amazement.
They sang and shouted, celebrating how great God is!

God was preparing the dark and formless earth as a place for life.
As God's Spirit moved above the waters, God spoke...and creation took shape.

God made light—pushing back the darkness...
Then God...divided the oceans from the sky...
and gathered the waters, so dry land would surface...

God made plants, flowers, and trees grow—all with seeds in them so they could reproduce themselves. Water rose from the ground to nourish these plants.

Then God created the sun, the moon, and the universe around...
and set seasons and time into motion...

And God filled the seas with fish, the sky with birds,
and the earth with all kinds of wild animals.

Looking at all of this wonderful creation, God thought, *This is really good!*

Then God decided to create another being, one lower than the angels.
And God said, "We'll make humans in our image—to be like us.
They'll take care of the earth and everything that lives there."

So God took dirt from the earth and formed the first human.
When God breathed breath into the human's nostrils, he suddenly came to life!
This first human would be known as Adam, meaning, "from the earth."

God placed Adam in a beautiful garden, surrounded by all kinds of delicious fruit so he'd never go hungry.

God gave him great responsibility—to work in the garden and care for everything that lived there.
God even brought all of the animals right to Adam so he could give them names.

In the center of this garden were two special trees—a Tree of Life and a tree giving Knowledge of Good and Evil. God told Adam, "Enjoy the fruit from every tree in this garden, except for one; if you eat from the Tree of the Knowledge of Good and Evil, you will definitely die." (Pause)

Then God said to Adam, "It's not good for you to be alone. I'll create a partner to compliment you." So God caused Adam to fall into a deep sleep, removed one of his ribs, then closed up his side where it was taken from.

God used Adam's rib to form the first woman.
When God brought her to Adam, Adam shouted, "At last!"
Adam would call his new companion Eve, meaning "giver of life."

Adam and Eve united together as one—joined as husband and wife. And God told them to continue creating by having children.

Although Adam and Eve were naked, they never felt ashamed.

So both the man and woman were created to reflect God's own image.

And God would come and walk with them in the cool of the day. They lived under God's care and protection—a life that was whole and complete.

After creating all of this, God thought, *This is excellent in every way!*
Then God rested and set aside a day in each week for humans to rest and enjoy being with God.

3. RETELL THE STORY

For For specific retelling ideas see Appendix B or go to the ideas section on www.echoth-estory.com. You should introduce the symbol for "creation" during the retelling to help participants place a visual identifier with this story.

GROUP RETELLING EXAMPLE:

LEADER: *Before we share our observations and questions about the story, we're going to do a Group Retelling. This basically means everyone in this group is going to help put the events of the story together, in order.*

I want you to describe the events from the story we just heard—not from other versions you have read or heard—so we can all focus on the same thing. Okay?

What happened at the very beginning of the story?

FOLLOW-UP QUESTIONS AND HINTS... (use these ONLY if the group gets stuck...)

The story began with God forming the earth...
- Who was there watching God? How did the angels respond?

Then God took the formless earth and transformed it into a place for life...
- What did God create? Anything else?
- What do you remember about the plants and trees?
- How did God feel about these created things?

Then God created another being...
- Who would this being be like?
- How did God create this first human?
- What responsibilities did God give Adam?
- How did the animals get their names?

Next, the story describes two trees...
- What do you remember about these two trees?

Then God decides to create a different kind of human...
- What happened? How did God do this?
- How did Adam respond?

Toward the end of the story it describes Adam and Eve's relationship with God...
- What was their relationship like?

- When would Adam and Eve walk with God?

- Are there any other details that we are forgetting?

What happens at the very end of the story?

LEADER: You did a great job in the retelling!

4. DIALOGUE ABOUT THE STORY
Make sure you establish guidelines for the storying dialogue. Go to Appendix B or the ideas section on www.echothestory.com for specific examples to set up your dialogue time.
- The questions in italics are for follow-up—use as time allows and as needed.

- You can help your group focus by gently asking, "Where did you see that in the story?"

DIALOGUE QUESTIONS:
- How did you picture the world (or garden) God created in this story? ...what did you see, hear, and smell? *...how did this story make you feel?*

- What was one thing you noticed in this story for the first time?
  What did this story make you wonder about? What questions did it bring up?

- What kind of relationship did God have with humans?
  Where did you see that in the story?
  How did God communicate with the humans?

- What do you think the daily conversations between God and the humans were like?
  What do you think they talked about?
  This story tells us that Adam and Eve experienced "a life that was whole and complete." The Hebrew word to describe this is shalom. *What do you think a life of shalom with God is like?*

- How are humans unique from all of the other creatures God made?

  Who were humans created to reflect?

  How do you think we are like God? ...unlike God?

  What responsibilities did God give the humans?

  Why do you think God gave them responsibilities?

  What do you think it means for us to take care of God's creation?

- What kind of relationship did Adam and Eve have with each other?

  What did Adam say when he first saw Eve? How do you think he felt?

  Why do you think Adam and Eve were not ashamed of being naked?

- What do you think is the significance of the two trees in the center of the garden?

  What might they tell us about God? ...about the humans?

  Why do you think humans were created with limitations?

  Why do you think God gave us the ability to choose?

  What was God risking by doing this? What was to gain?

- What are we learning about humans from this story?

  ...from their relationship with God?

  ...from their relationship with each other?

  ...from their relationship with creation?

  How might this story give us a glimpse of our true identities?

An Idea for Leaders

Make a list of what you're noticing about God and humans—add to and revisit the list after each story. This will help your group make connections between the stories.

- What are we learning about God from this story?

  ...from what God created?

  ...from how the angels responded to God?

  ...from God's relationship with the humans?

  ...from the responsibilities God gave the humans?

  ...from what God did at the very end of the story (rest)?

5. CONNECT THE STORY TO YOUR LIFE

You may want to break your group into groups of three for more in-depth discussion and prayer. Consider asking participants to write down their response before sharing in their groups.

- What does it mean for YOU to be created in God's image?

  How should that change they way you live?

  How should that change the way you view yourself?

Additional Connection Questions (optional):

- Based on this story, what do you think God desires from us?

- In what ways can you break the rhythm of your week, rest, and enjoy God on the "sabbath"?

- How might you get better at caring for God's creation and helping others to do the same?

FOR FURTHER EXPLORATION:

Ask participants to read and reflect on Genesis 1-2, Psalm 8, and Psalm 104 this week. Next time you gather, share your new observations together!

APPENDIX D:
A SUMMARY NARRATIVE OF THE BIBLE

SEEING THE BIG PICTURE

There are a variety of ways to see the panorama of God's story. One way is to look at God's Story is as a series of episodes. An episode is a distinct event that's a part of a greater whole… like a chapter in a book or a scene from a movie. The following episodes will help give us a big picture of God's story and allow us to see more clearly God's desire to restore his relationship with us.

| CREATION | SEPARATION | PROMISE | GOD-WITH-US | DEATH TO LIFE | THE CHURCH | NEW CREATION |

* God is represented by the Greek letter *Theta* "Θ", sometimes used to abbreviate *Theós*, meaning "God."

** The circle around the symbols represents a whole and complete relationship with God.

BIBLE SUMMARY NARRATIVE:

This story begins as the Creator of all, God, was preparing the earth as a place for life. God filled the earth with plants and all kinds of creatures. The most special of these creatures were human begins, formed in God's own likeness…*in God's image.*

God entrusted the humans to care for the earth and all of **creation**. God walked closely with them, showing them the best possible way to live. Under God's reign, the humans lived a life that was whole and complete.

In spite of this close relationship, the humans rebelled, choosing to live their own way over God's. Living outside of God's reign brought great consequences. Now **separated** from God, humans became subject to sickness, pain, and death.

Soon, humans spiraled out of control, acting out in selfishness and violence against one another. Determined to restore his creation, God chose a man named Abraham and his descendants to be a special **people**. God made a *covenant* with them, **promising** that they would extend God's blessing and restoration to the entire world!

These special people, called the Israelites, were called to live differently, showing the world what it means to live closely with God. God gave them a beautiful land where they enjoyed great blessings and grew into a large nation.

But it wasn't long before the Israelites chose to live their own way over God's. In their rebellion the Israelites encountered great struggles and became slaves of other nations. But God continued to give his people hope, promising to send a rescuer to break the power of their selfishness and rebellion.

Enter a man named Jesus. His life, teaching, and miracles all proved he was who he said he was: God's son in human form...***God-with-us!*** Jesus lived a remarkable life, always choosing to live God's way. He called people to follow him, inviting them to be a part of the "Kingdom of God" and live under God's reign once again.

Jesus chose a surprising way to help humans be restored to God—because he'd lived perfectly, God allowed Jesus to become our substitute and take on the required punishment for all of humanity's rebellion. After suffering a brutal **death**, Jesus came **back to life** three days later and was seen by more than 500 eyewitnesses. The power of selfishness and rebellion was conquered once and for all!

Jesus challenged his followers to live as he did and sent God's Spirit to live inside of them and empower them. This was the beginning of **The Church**—a community of people across the globe who follow Jesus in living God's way and share in God's mission to restore the world.

This story continues with us. We are called to be The Church—a new kind of community that'll show the world what it means to live in God's reign...returning to the life we were created for.

The end of this amazing story lies ahead. Jesus promised to return one day and bring about God's **new creation**. God's reign will come in fullness, restoring all things to the way God designed them. *Until then, may we live in God's ways, giving people a glimpse of what life is like in the coming Kingdom.*

INTERACTION:

As you read or listened to this narrative what did you picture in your mind?

What did this summary help you notice for the first time about God's Story?

What do you think God's Story is ultimately about?

How do you think looking at God's entire story at once is helpful?

How does this story continue right now? How are we a part of it?

APPENDIX E:
A BRIEF HISTORY OF CHRONOLOGICAL BIBLE STORYING
by Dr. Grant Lovejoy

The newest part of the phrase "Chronological Bible Storying" (CBS) is the "Bible" part. The word *Bible*, derived from the Greek word *biblia*, meaning "books," actually came into use long after storytelling and chronology were part of Israel's life. The books of Moses, for instance, were written no sooner than 700 years after God called Abram to leave Ur and go to the place God would show him. Presumably Abraham's descendants preserved those stories and their chronology by oral means until they were finally written down in books. Then Christians eventually gathered the inspired writings into compilations called "Bibles" and the Christian church received them as Scripture. CBS focuses on telling these inspired stories from Scripture, not fictional stories, illustrations, and the like. So it should be clear that the individual components of CBS are ancient. But the way they've been blended together in CBS is a much more recent development.

Historically, some individual missionaries used strategies with similarities to CBS. For example, Hans Rudi Weber's *The Communication of the Gospel to Illiterates*[1] describes his efforts to use stories and chalk drawings to teach illiterates in what is today Indonesia. But the work of Trevor McIlwain in the 1970s is the beginning of what became CBS.[2] McIlwain worked with New Tribes Missions (NTM) in the Philippines. He tried a number of approaches with a tribal group who had previously professed faith in Christ, but had reverted to many of their old ways and beliefs. Eventually McIlwain chose to teach chronologically through the Bible, starting with Genesis. Each session started with a focus on the biblical story, then shifted to expository teaching. This chronological Bible exposition produced a much stronger understanding of God's nature and the Christian faith within the people and transformed their lives. McIlwain named this approach "Chronological Bible Teaching."[3]

McIlwain's success attracted the attention of other missionaries working in the Philippines, including Bill Tisdale and Jim Slack of the Foreign Mission Board (FMB—later International Mission Board) of the Southern Baptist Convention (SBC). Slack had read Weber's book on communicating with illiterates in a doctoral seminar at Southwestern Baptist Theological Seminary. He recognized the value of what McIlwain was doing. So he invited McIlwain to teach his approach to two large groups of Baptist missionaries and national leaders. But after hearing McIlwain's presentation, Slack and others in both the FMB and NTM concluded that McIlwain's approach was too literate. It was not reproducible among most Filipino church leaders.

So New Tribes missionaries Dell and Sue Schultze, Les Plett, Jay Jackson, and Tom Steffen began experimenting with and adapting McIlwain's approach. So did Slack and several SBC missionaries. The five New Tribes missionaries retained the chronological and biblical emphases, but reduced the amount of expository teaching somewhat and emphasized storytelling. Dell and Sue Schultze subsequently produced their own set of stories and teaching approaches, which they published as *God and Man*.[4] Tom Steffen later wrote *Reconnecting God's Story to Ministry: Cross-Cultural Storytelling at Home and Abroad*[5] to urge missionaries to recover this lost art. This group of approaches is sometimes called Chronological Bible Storytelling because it's more narrative and less expositional than McIlwain's approach. But they retained varying degrees of expositional teaching in the story and the instruction that followed the story.

By the late 1980s, Jim Slack concluded that existing approaches to chronological Bible presentation were too literate for use with oral communicators. He began working on a form of chronological Bible presentation that utilized storytelling followed by dialogue. He carefully avoided including exposition in either the story or the dialogue. After becoming a church growth consultant for the SBC International Mission Board (IMB), Slack enlisted J. O. Terry to join him in developing the approach. Terry, a media specialist, had used storying in the Philippines as well. Together they refined the methodology that has now been endorsed by the IMB leadership. In an effort to differentiate it from the approaches of McIlwain and the others, Slack and Terry called their approach "storying."

In the 1990s Slack and Terry continued to revise the approach while introducing it to Southern Baptist missionaries and national partners in numerous workshops around the world. In 1992 the IMB leadership authorized Slack to approach Southwestern Baptist Theological Seminary for assistance in critiquing, developing, and teaching CBS. Because its leaders believed the issues involved were primarily communicational, the IMB approached the preaching department rather than the missions department at Southwestern. Through this contact they were invited to teach CBS in a course at Southwestern Baptist Theological Seminary in 1994. In the 1994–95 academic year, Southwestern Seminary granted [Dr. Lovejoy] a sabbatical leave to study CBS and associated academic issues. Beginning in 1995, [he] joined Slack and Terry in leading some of the storying workshops.

From the brief history set forth above, it should be evident that it was concerns about literacy that caused Slack, and later Terry, to develop storying in the way that they did. When they began to delve into the extensive literature on orality and literacy, it became evident that Western missionaries were up against a powerful communicational barrier that was (and still is) invisible to most literate missionaries.

*Excerpted from "Chronological Bible Storying: Description, Rationale and Implications," a paper presented at the Non-Print Media Consultation in Nairobi, Kenya, June 2000. Prepared by Dr. Grant Lovejoy, used with permission.

NOTES

1   London: SCM, 1957. See also Herbert V. Klem, *Oral Communication of the Scripture* (Pasadena, Cal.: William Carey Press, 1982).

2   The following historical review is drawn largely from James B. Slack and J. O. Terry, *Chronological Bible Storying: A Methodology for Presenting the Gospel to Oral Communicators*, March 1999 ed. (Richmond, Va.: International Mission Board of the SBC, 1999).

3   See Trevor McIlwain, *Building on Firm Foundations* and others in his multi-volume set of books.

4   Dell G. Schultze and Rachel Sue Schultze, *God and Man* (Manila: Privately published, 1984; rev. ed., 1987; Manila: Church Strengthening Ministry, 1994).

5   LaHabra, Cal.: Center for Organizational and Ministry Development, 1996.

APPENDIX F:
BIBLE STORYING IN AFRICA
By John Witte

INTRODUCTION:

John Witte is the person who first introduced me to Bible Storying. He inspired and challenged me to pursue this powerful approach to the Scriptures within a North American context. The following story was transcribed from an interview I did with John in April 2008 for www.echothestory.com.—*Michael Novelli*

JOHN'S STORY ON STORYING:

My ministry training was a typical seminary education, based on exegesis of the text. I loved that stuff and I still do—it really has formed me in a lot of ways.

In 1990 when my family moved to Kenya, I did a lot of preaching to youth groups and larger churches. People there seemed to respond well to this expository type of preaching, but after some time, I realized that only a few of them could reproduce it. I could show off in front of them, in a sense, and it made me feel good, but it wasn't impacting their lives in terms of them being able to take any of it into ministry themselves.

In 1991, I was introduced to Chronological Bible Storying by Dr. Jim Slack, a member of our missions board. Dr. Slack was traveling around the world introducing missionaries to this method of teaching people the Scriptures through story and dialogue. When I first heard about this method, I was pretty biased against it because of my love for exegesis and propositional teaching.

I tried storying a few times, and found that the African people responded well to this. In a two-day meeting with the Mossai on the Kenya / Tanzania border, I told about 25 stories in Ke-Swahelia and they translated them into Ke-Mossai or Ke-Mo. Even though I was really lousy at it, they loved it!

In spite of some of my positive experiences, I seemed to always return to my expository ways of preaching. It wasn't until years later in Kesumo that I made the conscious decision to communicate using storying and oral strategies appropriate in the African context. I realized I must take what I'd learned in seminary and ministry and bend it like a sapling toward the people in order to serve and reach them. I had to learn how to communicate in a whole new way, and to redefine my whole approach—communication became a way to serve to the people I lived among.

I really was pretty bad at storying to begin with, but I kept working hard at it. After some time, a neat thing happened; not only were the stories well received in African settings, but also in the state side churches when I came back home. I would travel and tell people of how storying was working overseas, then led them through Bible narratives. People just loved it.

After seeing how people in completely different cultures and continents connected with storying, I was completely convinced that this was the better way, the preferred way to communicate our Christian and biblically-based message to people.

The best experience I had with using oral stragies—storying, dance, drama, and music—was with the Karamojong in north east Uganda, specifically with the Dodoth. In 2003 when I began working with them, I had four years of experience with storying full-time, and I wanted to apply it in that setting.

The Dodoth are what you might picture tribal African people are...very isolated and quite proud of their culture. They are pastoralists, a cattle-based culture. Because of the civil war in Sudan, many of them had AK-47 weapons and were constantly raiding one another for cattle. You needed cattle to acquire more wives, and the more wives and the more sons from those wives you had was the way you showed power, wealth, and manhood in that culture. I was moving in and among a very primitive people.

When I began storying with them, I worked hard at making the stories simpler so they would be more accessible. I also sought out those in the tribe who were very gifted in Karamojong music and dance. They are a culture that is centered around music and dance—that is the way they enjoy life and express joy. Every night they have the potential to be raided for cattle, so the men stay up around the campfire until 2:00 A.M., when it would be too late for intruders to steal and drive their cattle back before daybreak. They live a harsh life, where no one goes out after dark because it is so dangerous. So music and dance were an incredible release for these people.

After I would teach them the biblical narratives, they would put the stories to their own music. Then, we would go to different villages nearby and lead the people in storying, then one of the locals would teach the songs for the stories we shared. They already recognized the music and instantly embraced this approach. In twenty or thirty minutes, they were ready to perform the songs they just heard! I also added drama to the storying process with the Karamojong from time to time, and they really liked it! For oral people, drama is a form of interpretation—when they see the story dramatized they have to think through it again and process what really happened. I could tell by the way the people in this region were responding that they felt like, "I can do this, I can be involved in this story and give this away to others."

We did not build any structures or church buildings; we would just sit on rock out-croppings near the village, telling stories, singing and dancing. These outcroppings were strategic locations providing a place to hide behind rocks and shoot at potential intruders.

We got lots of invitations from other tribes, so we would walk all over the region sharing songs and dramas to introduce people to the story. Song and dance was a like a wave coming in off the ocean with storying coming in behind it to shore it up.

In the south Sudan we also did storying among the Jure—a people who are perhaps more primitive than the Karamojong. The men wear leather loincloths and the women cover themselves with green leaves with a black tail hanging down the back.

We were working with an existing Bible school there, helping train up indigenous leaders. Most of the students were unable to read. One day we got into a discussion with the students about how we can take God's message to other people. The students immediately started chiming in, "You teach us differently than our teachers do. When you teach us, we really understand it."

I responded, "Don't judge your teachers too harshly; they are trying and doing the best they know how to do." I said this because I knew they were being taught through western classroom models focused on proposition and systematic theology, of which I had done years of that kind of teaching in Kenya.

Some of the students continued, "When were were on break we went home and sang the songs and danced and these little old women came around and joined us. (In their culture they would dance by moving their feet back and forth while they quickly clapped their hands.) These old women loved it—as long as we would sing and dance they would stay around—when we stopped they would leave. Later on these old woman came back and said to us, "Those are really good songs; what do those songs mean?"

So we told them the stories of what those songs mean. When we finished, the old women said to us, "For the first time in our lives, now we understand what the Bible means."

I have goose bumps thinking about this...when I heard the students share this story, I realized that storying and oral teaching methods were not just theory. These were the most under-resourced, under-cared for, forgotten people in the middle of nowhere. They had little or no access to westernization or Scripture, and now they were saying, "Ah ha, now we get it."

APPENDIX G:
SOMA: A STORY-FORMED COMMUNITY
by Caesar Kalinowski, cofounder of Echo and
elder at Soma in Tacoma, Washington

When we began storying at Soma, our leaders were powerfully impacted by how simple and yet profound the stories were. Most of them had been around the Bible and Christianity for years, if not all of their lives, yet somehow this was changing them. The Story was implicating them in new ways. *If this is who God is and what God has been up to...and if this is what God has always desired for his people...how should we live and love within our city?* They were beginning to find that their lives are a part of the Story; the Story is still being written, and they're in the unfolding chapters.

We then trained these leaders so they could reproduce the process with others in their small, home-based, missional communities that were newly forming. (Missional communities are what we call our small groups of people gathered specifically around the mission of God.) I remember sitting in on one of our group nights and listening to the interactions. There was quite a mix of people in this group—everyone from a seminary graduate, to young people (both single and married with kids), and even a couple who were self-proclaimed agnostics. The leader of this group shared the story of Cain and Abel and then began to ask casual but intentional questions. The dialogue went on effortlessly but passionately for more than an hour.

Everyone interacted on an equal level, informed by the narrative itself, not previous Bible knowledge. This process of studying the Word seems to be a great "leveler," allowing everyone to participate freely. I'd never seen such freedom of thought displayed within a "Bible study," especially by folks with such different backgrounds and experiences in life.

My favorite part was when the one woman, an agnostic, gently (and correctly) cleaned up some of the group members' thinking concerning the idea of human "choice" from something she recalled from a previous story the group had discussed weeks earlier. It was awesome to watch her actually *teach* all of us in a natural and, I believe, Spirit-guided way. This woman's faith and bond with our community and with God grew rapidly and authentically over the weeks that followed. We literally watched this woman and her husband change before our eyes. The times of interaction around the Story and within a loving community transformed their lives.

We continue to start new missional communities using Chronological Bible Storying. We've found that many, if not most, Christians don't have a strong biblical theology. So much of what they've learned has been a systematic approach to studying the Bible—and devoid of context. It's sort of like looking at an object through a microscope without knowing what the object is beforehand. Do you remember looking through a microscope at something that looked like a mountain range and then pulling back the lens to reveal that what you were seeing was actually a small piece of a fingernail or an onion skin? That's somewhat like the way many of us have been taught to understand the Bible. For instance, moralistic truths taken out of context and then applied to our lives aren't the most effective tools to study the Word of God.

As the church, we no longer have the luxury of speaking into a culture that has basic biblical understandings or points of reference. We have to start at the beginning and do so in a way that's understandable and reproducible. Teaching the Bible using story and dialogue has given us a way to immediately begin this process with others.

We continue to look for new ways to build community around Christ and to see many more people begin living out their true identities. I cannot imagine doing this without the gift of storying. I'm truly thankful to be a part of this story-formed family of missionaries who serve God in Tacoma. The Story of God has gripped us and continues to make disciples who make disciples. To hear more about what God is doing in and through our community, go to www.somachurch.com.

APPENDIX H:
ECHO'S WORKSHOPS & MERGE STUDENT EVENTS

HELP YOUR STUDENTS FIND THEMSELVES IN A GREATER STORY

A Weeklong Experience Inspiring Your High School Students to:

> Experience God's Story in a new and deeper way through: creative storytelling / art and media / discussion groups / interactive experiences

> Realize how this story connects together and continues with them

> Discover their unique part in this story and allow it to shape their lives

MERGE   www.mergeevent.com

HOST A BIBLE STORYING WORKSHOP!

DURING THIS SIX-HOUR WORKSHOP YOU AND YOUR TEAM WILL...

> Discover new things about God and the Bible through a "Storying" experience.

> Learn new methods to communicate and interact with God's Story.

> Practice skills for leading a Storying and dialogue session.

> Get practical ideas and resources to help you lead in your context.

Download a sample workshop schedule at www.echothestory.com.

CUSTOMIZED EXPERIENCES, WORKSHOPS & CONSULTING

We can help you create a experience that helps people engage in God's Story in powerful ways. Contact us to help you plan your next event or training.

We provide workshops and consulting in: creativity, experiential learning, event programming, curriculum design, and learner-centered teaching.

APPENDIX I:
RECOMMENDED STORYING RESOURCES

For updated lists and reviews of some of these resources go to www.echothestory.com

IN PRINT:

>> COMMUNICATION / LEARNING

Beyond Smells and Bells: The Wonder and Power of Christian Liturgy
Mark Galli (Paraclete Press, Brewster, MA, 2008)

Collaborative Learning Techniques
Elizabeth F. Barkley, K. Patricia Cross, and Claire Howell Major
(Jossey Bass, San Francisco, CA, 2005)

Experiential Learning: Experience as the Source of Learning and Development
David A. Kolb (Prentice Hall, Upper Saddle River, NJ, 1984)

From Telling to Teaching: A Dialogue Approach to Adult Learning
Joye A. Norris (Learning By Dialogue, North Myrtle Beach, SC, 2003)

How to Ask Great Questions: Guide Your Group to Discovery with These Proven Techniques
Karen Lee-Thorp (NavPress, Colorado Springs, CO, 1998).

Informal Learning: Rediscovering the Natural Pathways That Inspire Innovation and Performance
Jay Cross (Pfeiffer, San Francisco, CA, 2006)

Learner Centered Teaching: Five Key Changes to Practice
Maryellen Weimer (Jossey Bass, San Francisco, CA, 2002)

Orality and Literacy: The Technologizing of the Word
Walter J. Ong (Routledge Press, Florence, KY, 1982)

The Art of Storytelling: Easy Steps to Presenting an Unforgettable Story
John Walsh (Moody Press, Chicago, IL, 2003)

The Storyteller's Start-Up Book: Finding, Learning, Performing and Using Folktales
Margaret Read MacDonald (August House, Little Rock, AR, 1993)

The Way They Learn: How to Discover and Teach to Your Child's Strengths
Cynthia Ulrich Tobias (Tyndale House Publishing, Wheaton, IL, 1994)

The Medium Is the Massage: An Inventory of Effects
Marshall McLuhan and Quentin Fiore (Gingko Press, Corte Madera, CA, New Ed. 2005)

Workshops: Designing and Facilitating Experiential Learning
Jeff E. Brooks-Harris, Susan R., Stock-Ward
(Sage Publications,Thousand Oaks, CA, 1999)

>> BIBLE STORYTELLING / NARRATIVE THEOLOGY

Christ Plays in Ten Thousand Places: A Conversation in Spiritual Theology
Eugene H. Peterson (Eerdmans, Grand Rapids, MI, 2005)

Experiential Storytelling: (Re) Discovering Narrative to Communicate God's Message
Mark Miller (Youth Specialties, San Diego, CA, 2003)

Making Disciples of Oral Learners
Avery Willis & Steve Evans (Elim Publishing, Lima, NY, 2005)

Our Father Abraham: Jewish Roots of the Christian Faith
Marvin R. Wilson (Eerdmans Publishing, Grand Rapids MI, 1989)

Preaching Re-Imagined: The Role of the Sermon in Communities of Faith
Doug Pagitt (Zondervan,Grand Rapids, MI, 2005)

Story Journey; An Invitation to the Gospel as Storytelling
Thomas E. Boomershine (Abingdon Press, Nashville, TN, 1988)

Tell Me a Story: The Life-Shaping Power of Our Stories
Daniel Taylor (Bog Walk Press, St. Paul, MN, 2001)

The Art of Biblical Narrative
Robert Alter (Basic Books, Cambridge MA, 1981)

The God-Hungry Imagination: The Art of Storytelling for Postmodern Youth Ministry
Sarah Arthur (Upper Room Books, Nashville TN, 2007)

The Steward Living in Covenant: A New Perspective on Old Testament Stories
Ronald E. Vallet (Eerdmans, Grand Rapids, MI, 2001)

The Seventy Faces of Torah: The Jewish Way of Reading the Sacred Scriptures
Stephen M. Wylen (Paulist Press, Mahwah, NJ, 2005)

Thinking in Story: Preaching in a Post-Literate Age
Richard A. Jensen, (CSS Publishing, Lima, OH, 1995)

To Be Told: God Invites You to Co-Author Your Future
Dan Allender (WaterBrook Press, Colorado Springs, CO, 2006)

>> BIBLE STORIES AND OVERVIEWS

A Walk through the Bible
Leslie Newbigin (Regent College Publishing, Vancourver, BC, 1999)

Creation to Revelation: A Brief Account of the Biblical Story
James O. Chatham (Eerdmans, Grand Rapids, MI, 2006)

God's Big Picture: Tracing the Storyline of the Bible
Vaughan Roberts (Inter-Varsity Press, Downers Grove IL, 2002)

God's EPIC Adventure: Changing Our Culture by the Story We Live and Tell
Winn Griffin (Harmon Press, Woodinville, WA 2007)

GodStories: New Narratives from Sacred Texts
H. Stephen Shoemaker (Judson Press,Valley Forge, 1998)

Telling God's Story: The Biblical Narrative from Beginning to End
Preben Vang and Terry Carter (Broadman & Holman, Nashville, TN, 2006)

Telling the Truth: The Gospel as Tragedy, Comedy and Fairy Tale
Frederick Buechner (Harper Collins, 1977)

The Big Story: What Actually Happens in the Bible
Nick Page (Authentic Media, Carlisle UK, 2007)

The Drama of Scripture: Finding Our Place in the Biblical Story
Craig Bartholomew & Michael Goheen (Baker Academic, Ada, MI 2004)

The Story of Stories
Karen C. Hinkley, (Navpress,Colorado Springs, CO, 1991)

The Story We Find Ourselves In: Further Adventures of a New Kind of Christian
Brian D. McLaren (Jossey Bass, San Francisco, CA, 2003)

The Unfolding Drama of the Bible
Bernhard W. Anderson (Augsburg Fortress, Minneapolis MN, 2006)

>> BIBLES AND COMMENTARIES

The Message
Eugene H. Peterson (NavPress, Colorado Springs, CO, 2003)

The Narrated Bible in Chronological Order
F. Lagard Smith (Harvest House, Eugene, OR, 1984)

The New Living Translation (NLT)
(Tyndale House, Carol Stream, IL, 1996)

The Story: Read the Bible as One Seamless Story from Beginning to End
31 Narratives from Today's New International Version
(Zondervan, Grand Rapids, MI 2005)

The Storyteller's Companion to the Bible
Commentary Series – several volumes available
(Abingdon Press, Nashville, TN 1984-2001)

ON THE WEB:

Christian Storytelling Network – www.christianstorytelling.com

Chronological Bible Storying – www.chronologicalbiblestorying.com/

Echo – My Web site – www.echothestory.com

Following Jesus Missions Curriculum – www.fjseries.org

Imago Media – events, design & media – www.imagomedia.com

International Orality Network – www.oralbible.com

John Eldridge's Book Epic Reality – www.epicreality.com

Lego Bible Stories - meant for adults – www.thebricktestament.com

Merge High School Event – www.mergeevent.com

Network of Biblical Storytellers – www.nobs.org

OneStory Partnership – www.onestory.org

Online Bible Versions – www.biblegateway.com

OralStrategies – www.oralstrategies.com

PBS Storytellers – www.pbs.org/circleofstories

StoryRunners (Campus Crusade MIssions) – www.storyrunners.com

Storytelling Training by John Walsh – www.bibletelling.com

Quest One Story – www.thejavaclub.org

The Call of Story Presentation – www.callofstory.org

The Story of Jesus – www.hopenet.org/storjesus.html